WALKING
WITH
GOD

HOW A SIMPLE, DAILY HABIT
CAN CHANGE YOUR LIFE

JAMES WALLACE

www.southernriverpublishing.com

WALKING WITH GOD

Copyright © 2015 by James Wallace.

Scripture taken from the *HOLY BIBLE, NEW INTERNATIONAL VERSION,* Copyright © 1973, 1978, 1984 International Bible Society. Used by permission of Zondervan Bible Publishers. The actual edition from which I quote in this book, and the bible I've used since 1985, is The NIV Study Bible, Copyright © 1985 by The Zondervan Corporation. I've found the footnotes to be immensely valuable in deepening my understanding of scripture passages and providing context and cross-references.

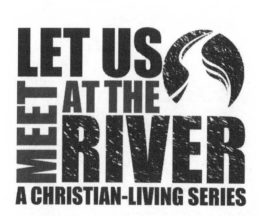

LET US
MEET AT THE
RIVER

A CHRISTIAN-LIVING SERIES

DEDICATION

To my wife, Nancy

God heard your prayers!

TABLE OF CONTENTS

INTRODUCTION

*Blessed are those who have learned to acclaim you,
who walk in the light of your presence, O Lord.*

- Psalm 89:15

T his book is about the transformational power of something very simple. Something that almost all of us can do, every day.

Walking!

Not just any walking. I'm talking about walking outside, along the most inspirational routes you can reasonably find, wherever you live. And not just walking outside along a scenic route. Those things are just the "ingredients" that help create something amazing: positive benefits that impact your daily living, and transformation that can change your life –

spiritually, emotionally, and mentally. How is that possible, from simply walking?

Because it's not just walking.

It's walking with God.

I started off "just walking."

Then something else began to happen.

In this book, I'll share with you exactly what happened, and show you how you, too, can create your own, unique walks with God – walks that will transform your life in amazing ways – and impact the lives of others, even beyond your lifetime.

David Eifrig is a medical doctor and financial newsletter writer. At the beginning of each year he publishes a list of the top ways to improve your health during the year (as a bonus report of *Retirement Millionaire*, published by Stansberry & Associates). First on his 2014 list (second on his 2015 list, after sleep) was *movement.* Here's a portion of what he said:

Movement offers dozens of benefits, more than just keeping you at a healthy weight. Regular exercise reduces stress, releases endorphins, improves brain function, and improves cardiovascular health.

And here's the GREAT news . . . you don't have to engage in strenuous exercise . . . Light exercise (walking is my favorite) for about 20 to 30 minutes a day gives you nearly all the benefits, while avoiding injuries like muscle strains and joint pain.

In the process of "moving" and "getting healthy" I noticed other things happening:

Awareness.

Observation.

Reflection.

Thinking.

Focus.

Spiritual, emotional, and mental energy.

Renewal.

Transformation.

If this sounds too transcendental, don't panic. I have never done sit-still meditation, yoga, tai chi, or any similar activity. Thousands of people do, and the science and data show the benefits of those pursuits. I've seen many articles recently on the benefits of meditation, in particular. It's #5 on Dr. Eifrig's 2015 list. But for those of us not yet masters of meditation, it's nice to realize that simple, old-school walking can yield equal and perhaps even deeper benefits.

The "spiritual energy" described in this book is drawn from a Christian perspective. I walk alone, early in the morning. Some of the non-physical benefits of my walks are probably associated with a type of meditation, or are similar to those produced by meditation. I just know that, for me, walking along a scenic path is fun and interesting, but sitting still in a lotus position seems like a mild form of torture. Most people who meditate likely also walk or do some other "movement" exercise, so the two are certainly not mutually exclusive. The more the merrier.

For those of you walking now, thinking about walking, or not thinking about it but physically able to walk, this book's for you.

I describe my walks and the unexpected things that began to happen during them. I feel compelled to share my story, in the hope that it will provide encouragement and inspiration to others and be a "point of light" that will help a thousand other lights shine more brightly.

You'll discover how walking can be an amazing way to create spiritual, emotional, and mental "energy" that you can tap throughout the day – and for a lifetime. If you are already experiencing this energy in your walks, I hope you find camaraderie with my experience and use it as affirmation and motivation to stay the course and spread the good news.

When I was editing the manuscript of this book, an issue of Dr. Micozzi's *Insiders' Cures* health newsletter popped into my inbox. One of the articles got my immediate attention: "How you can get a younger, healthier brain in less than 30 minutes."

Wow. Really? The article discussed two recent research studies that showed "mindfulness meditation" (in as little as two months) increased the participants' "grey matter" and (over a longer period) "thickened their cerebral cortexes."

What does that mean? The meditation was creating more brain cells and changing the structure of the brain. The meditators had enhanced cognitive abilities. Their brains were growing, not shrinking. They were reversing the aging of their brains. "Mindfulness meditation," in essence, is a *Benjamin Button* for the brain.

What is "mindfulness meditation?" I had not heard that term before reading the article. Here is Dr. Micozzi's explanation:

> *The essence of mindfulness meditation is being "present." Not thinking ahead to the future or back to the past. But just being fully aware of everything in the moment. So practicing it is simple.*

That's exactly what I do when I walk! (See the next chapter.) I have been "mindfully meditating" without even knowing it. I am "in the moment" while walking – I've combined a type of meditation with walking.

So now we have a perfect trifecta: physical exercise/ health benefits + spiritual/emotional/mental energy + a bigger, smarter, younger brain. That's as good as it gets!

Let's get walking!

CHAPTER ONE

LET'S ALL GO DOWN
TO THE RIVER

There is a river whose streams make glad the city of God, the holy place where the Most High dwells.

God is within her, she will not fall; God will help her at break of day.

- Psalm 46:4-5

"Let's All Go Down to the River" is a Christian gospel song. The rendition by Etta James is one of my favorite songs. If you haven't heard it, I encourage you to listen to it today. For two more good songs of the river, listen to "Down by the Riverside" (Etta James) and "Down in the River to Pray" (Alison Krauss).

I like the imagery of a river, for three reasons.

One, it has been physically accurate for my walks. When I wrote the manuscript for this book, I lived in Natchez, Mississippi. It's the oldest town on the Mississippi River, founded in 1716 when the French established Fort Rosalie on a bluff overlooking the river. My walking path was through the downtown "garden district" (the oldest section of town, replete with homes and buildings dating from 1790), down to the bluff along the river, along the walkway at the edge of the bluff, and then back through the garden district. So literally, I walked down to the big river. I like history and architecture, so there were many interesting things to see on the way down to the river.

Two, it evokes emotion. I drew inspiration from walks along the river. The Mississippi is awesome to behold in all its size and power and in its relentless march to the sea. Truly, it is both an incredible example of God's creation and a reminder of His awesome power.

Three, it's metaphorical. Psalm 46:4-5 says there is a

river in the "city of God." The "city of God" refers to Jerusalem. Yet Jerusalem has no river. What, then, is the "river whose streams make glad the city of God?" The footnote in my NIV Study Bible explains:

[The river] serves as a metaphor for the continual outpouring of the sustaining and refreshing blessings of God, which make the city of God like the Garden of Eden.

What a powerful, vivid metaphor! This "river of blessings" metaphor has even more impact in the context of an actual, physical river. In the context of one of the largest rivers in the world, viewed panoramically from atop ancient bluffs nearly 200 feet above water's edge, this metaphor is as profound in its impact as any memorialized.

You probably don't have a river on your walking path. No matter. Your metaphorical river may be a lake, creek, beach, park, wooded lane, city sidewalk, hike and bike path, the streets in your subdivision, a dirt road in the country, a trail through a pasture, or something else. The point is to find the most visually enjoyable route you can, where you live, that is both safe and convenient. You may find several good routes.

How long should you walk? My Natchez walks took just under 40 minutes. I think anything from 30 minutes to an hour would work fine.

The walking path you choose should also be easy to navigate and relatively distraction-free. Let me explain. We just moved to a house on a lake, in the country. The small subdivision has a community trail along the waterfront. The roads within the subdivision are gravel. On my walks so far, I've battled large, dive-bombing flies. I've run into spider webs (nearly every day). I am constantly looking down, because the trail is rough, incomplete, and covered with weeds and limbs (but no snakes yet). I've found it hard to focus and get into the mindfulness-meditation mode on this portion of my walks. The portion on the quiet, paved road alongside the lake is fine.

The lake itself is very serene and plenty big. We recently got kayaks. My plan, beside having fun paddling around the lake and fishing with my family, is to see if I can re-create the benefits of my Natchez walks out on the water. If the plan works, I may write a sequel, *Kayaking with God* (seriously, something more like *Reflections on Lake Solitude*). For now, however, let's focus on walking.

Pick your optimal time to walk. Unless you are truly a night owl and live in Mayberry, I recommend walking in daylight hours. You can visually "absorb" your surroundings and maximize your other senses as well. That physical, sensory experience is part of the magic that elevates these walks onto other levels. If you can get up early, sunrise is hard to beat.

Many people walk in social groups. If that's you, try spending part of the walk in silence, to duplicate the benefits derived from walking solo. Who knows, your whole group may join in, so you still have a social experience and safety in numbers but can experience the "meditational" benefits described in this book. Some church groups are already doing what they call "faith walks."

If you listen to a playlist designed to pump you up and keep you moving fast, try unplugging or converting to jazz or classical music or another genre that doesn't drown out your ability to think and reflect. Keep the volume down. You can still "crank it up" on other parts of your workout. I walk pretty fast with no music.

Ok. You've got your setup.

You've picked a time of day to walk. By the way, make it the same time each day to the extent possible – it'll be much easier to establish the habit of daily walking, especially if you're just starting out or having trouble walking consistently. Walking at the same time each morning (within 15 minutes or so) really helps me stay on track. It becomes part of my routine.

You've got a scenic route (or the most interesting one you can find) to walk, and it's fairly easy to navigate, with minimal distractions.

You're walking alone or have made accommodations to allow for some focus time while walking with your group.

Now, start walking, and see what happens. No doubt

we will have some of the same experiences. But I'll bet you will also discover your own, unique revelations and insights that will impact how you function day-to-day and affect your life in larger ways.

What follows is what I've discovered on my walks, how these discoveries really apply to all of us, and how they can help each of us live a richer, better, more fulfilled life if we use the spiritual, emotional, and mental energies created to take action and make positive changes.

The best way to illustrate what I'm talking about is to "take you along" on a walk with me.

I will use my Natchez walks down to and along the Mississippi River.

CHAPTER TWO

EVERY DAY A BLESSING

So then, just as you received Christ Jesus as Lord, continue to live in him, rooted and built up in him, strengthened in the faith as you were taught, and overflowing with thankfulness.

- Colossians 2:6-7

Wake up, have a cup of coffee . . . and then step out the door into the early-morning light of another day. The first thing of which I become aware when walking is the sheer magnitude of God's blessings in my life. I think, wow, here I am, in this beautiful setting, alive, breathing, healthy, walking. God let me wake up and have another day!

How often do we take life for granted, as if it's understood it will always be there for us? As if the gift of life itself is as automatic and unconscious as a beating heart? Stepping outside, in the quiet morning stillness, makes me consciously aware of how lucky I am to be alive and have the ability to walk, both as a freedom we enjoy in this great country and as a physical attribute.

How many times do we fail to pause and reflect on the fact that we can still make an impact on our world, our loved ones, and accomplish the purposes for which God put us here? How many times do we take for granted the blessings in our lives? How many times do we fail to pause – even for a few minutes – and thank God for our lives, our health, our families?

The very first benefit of my daily walks, each time I step out the door, is this realization of blessing. Here I am, in the midst of God's creation. And it's wonderful.

As I . . .

. . . listen to birds singing their morning songs

. . . watch squirrels playing hide and seek

. . . feel the breeze on my face

. . . take in the faint smell of a distant wood fire

. . . look at the shifting shapes of a skyline formed by church steeples, pitched roofs, and old brick buildings

. . . watch clouds glowing pink from the sunrise

. . . see fog settled into the crevices of distant bluffs

. . . gaze at the calm, silent power of the water in the Mighty Mississippi rolling toward New Orleans

. . . I am filled with a feeling of deep gratitude for being allowed the privilege to experience such things.

I ponder my situation. I haven't been severely injured or killed in a car wreck. I don't have a deadly disease. I have the capacity to walk and walk fast. My family is all ok. We have peace in our country and city. We live in a beautiful town. My mind is sharp. My senses are acute. I have the ability to create.

Everything is a gift from God. I am here, today, by His grace. How often do we take credit for the positive things happening in our lives? My daily walks bring me back to an attitude of gratitude. They invariably reveal the depth of God's blessings, and that immediately brings a flush of thankfulness and humbleness.

My walks serve as a daily "course correction" for me. Remember, I began walking just for the physical exercise and cardio benefits. None of the other things that happened were mapped out in advance. They just happened. But now I am aware. As a result my focus seems sharper and greater.

During my walks, I am "in the moment." Every sense is on high alert. I have a feeling of calmness. Regrets of the past – which involve things we can't change – and worries about the future – which are exercises in futility – fade away in the glory of the present, the here, the now, the being, the living, the experiencing, the blessing of another day of life, and the gratitude that God has let it be so.

It's as if I've activated a machine that generates spiritual endorphins. And the machine gets stuck in high gear, producing enough of these energy packets to use during the day. I need them, so it's great to have them available. Sometimes they last an hour or two, sometimes the entire day. Sometimes beyond.

As you'll see, the intangible energy produced by the type of daily walks I describe in this book is so "high-value" that the inconvenience of waking up earlier, adjusting your schedule, putting one foot in front of the other on days you'd rather not, missing out on some other activity, and basically developing a new habit, will pale in comparison. In fact, the spiritual insights, the focus, the ideas, and the action plans you'll develop while walking will make the rest of your day much more productive than would have been the case if you'd skipped the walking time and used it for something else instead. Test this out!

The spiritual energy is the first production off the line of the machine. The contraption keeps on going, however, and produces mental and emotional energy also. What a great device! Like a big flywheel that keeps on spinning and generating electricity. Wish I could patent it. But the beauty of it is that anyone can tap it, because it's within each of us. You will create and experience it by your own walking, reflection, and observation. You will generate the sparks for your transformation and renewal.

What if negative things in our lives hinder us at times from feeling particularly blessed? What if those circumstances are so severe they make us wonder if God has tuned us out?

God tells us what to do:

But blessed is the man who trusts in the Lord, whose confidence is in him.

He will be like a tree planted by the water that sends out its roots by the stream.

It does not fear when heat comes; its leaves are always green.

It has no worries in a year of drought and never fails to bear fruit.

- Jeremiah 17:7-8

Though the pain and hurting are real, if we trust God,

He will breathe new life into us and lift our burdens. God will sustain and renew us with His living water – salvation through Christ, and the indwelling Holy Spirit.

So get out there and walk, even if (especially if) you are down. Focus your thoughts on God. Have confidence He is with you. Feel your heavy steps and heavy heart being lifted and lightened.

Remember God's goodness. Remember His greatness. That is what Asaph did when he was in extreme distress. He was so down and out he couldn't sleep or speak. He wondered if God had rejected him.

Will the Lord reject forever? Will he never show his favor again?

Has his unfailing love vanished forever? Has his promise failed for all time?

Has God forgotten to be merciful? Has he in anger withheld his compassion?

Then I thought, "To this I will appeal: the years of the right hand of the Most High."

I will remember the deeds of the Lord; yes, I will remember your miracles of long ago.

I will meditate on all your works and consider all your mighty deeds.

Your ways, O God, are holy. What god is so great as our God?

You are the God who performs miracles; you display your power among the peoples.

With your mighty arm you redeemed your people, the descendants of Jacob and Joseph.

- Psalm 77:7-15

When I step outside and see a beautiful sunrise over the water, I see God's handiwork. It's as if God paints a picture every morning, for us to enjoy – and to remind us of His greatness and presence. Look up. Look around. God is telling us, "Here I am." Use these moments to reflect on God's blessings in your life and thank Him.

CHAPTER THREE

THE WONDER OF A CHILD

But Jesus called the children to him and said, "Let the little children come to me, and do not hinder them, for the kingdom of God belongs to such as these. I tell you the truth, anyone who will not receive the kingdom of God like a little child will never enter it."

- Luke 18:16-17

I'm out the door, walking toward the river, seeing and sensing the immediate world around me, counting my and my family's blessings, and feeling an overwhelming sense of gratitude to God for everything good He's allowed to happen in my life. What then?

Well, the things described above don't just pop in and

pop out the first five minutes of the walk. They last. They linger. They continue to build, all the way to the river, and they seem to crest during my walk along the river bluff, which is the halfway point of my walk.

Children, especially toddlers and young children, are amazed by almost everything. They have an internal sense of wonder. The world is new, exciting, and magical. Lots of things are funny. They laugh at little things. Most of us have an inner child still within us. I think most adults repress it. Thankfully, mine has always been unrepressed.

According to conventional wisdom, in most settings adults are expected to be serious, dignified, and restrained. We are supposed to adhere to a set of rules and protocols that keep us safely within a box labelled "Normal Adult Behavior." Many (if not most) adults have conditioned themselves to stay quietly and politely inside the box. A civilized society, of course, requires norms of behavior and decorum for its adult citizenry. But that doesn't require us to switch off our imaginations at age 18 or 21. And it doesn't require us to be boring.

Various statistics on the internet indicate that children laugh 300 or more times a day, but adults only 10 to 20. Yikes! Who knows if those figures are accurate, but simple observation and common sense tell us that children laugh a lot more than adults and have more fun during the course of a day.

Children have great imaginations. Adults all too often stifle their imaginations. Over time, the imagination part of the average adult brain atrophies like an unused muscle. What a tragedy for adulthood. How depressing for us adults! We grow up and become dignifyingly boring and uncreative. (I may have just made up that word, "dignifyingly." If so, great!)

There's no rule that says we adults must always be staid and boring. We can make up stuff, just like kids turn a tree into a magical fortress . . . a stick into a magic wand or pirate's sword . . . a blanket over some chairs into a hidden cave or outlaw's hideout.

Join me in breaking the Law of Reverse Metamorphosis (I made that up), which says that as adults age they tend to lose the butterfly and gradually morph back into the caterpillar in the cocoon. Be the butterfly until you die! Smile more. Laugh more (a lot more). Spread your wings and explore. Be amazed at little things and big things. Let your walks – like mine for me – be a way for you to "grow younger" with each step, each new discovery.

My walks bring forth an inner-child sense of wonderment. As I walk, recognizing my blessings and being grateful for them, I find that my power of observation is heightened. Children notice birds, bugs, flowers, neat cloud shapes, unusual leaves and big trees, tugboats that look like the ones in the picture books that can talk, a man who looks like Santa Claus, cool rocks, colorful butterflies, sticks that could be swords or nun chucks, ants scurrying to and fro on a mound, and a hundred other things that adults, rushing to work or worrying about who knows what, miss. Not just miss, but are oblivious to.

I notice these things, just as a five-year old would. If you let them, they still create a sense of wonder even though you may be decades past your childhood. It's fun to slow down and observe. Each thing you'll see reinforces the amazing nature of the world in which we live. Many of the things will make you smile or even laugh. And all of them – different on each walk – make a fabric of life that weaves through the walk and enriches the experience. It makes me once again appreciate little things. It may add a year or more to my life, who knows.

Life extension or not, I know it's good to focus on simple pleasures and to smile and laugh. It's a great way to start the day. Never think you're too old or too cool to enjoy the little things that cross your path every day.

Back to my walks. What are some of the things I observe with wonder and delight? Here's a sampling. Notice that some are natural, while others are man-made. The natural things reinforce the wonder of God's creation and are a wellspring of spiritual and emotional energy. The man-made things can generate mental energy, as we'll see.

A morning symphony produced by the birds . . . every few blocks presents a different mix of melodies .

. . as if I'm walking through and hearing a playlist labeled "Nature."

A squirrel on a telephone pole playing hide and seek with me . . . two squirrels playing chase.

A huge, low cloud formation over the river that looks like the hand of God extending down to protect our community.

Six jet streams bursting through the sky, all from a central point.

The enormous volume of water in the Mississippi River rolling on, ever constant . . . the same way it's been doing for eons.

The incredible vista along the Natchez bluffs of the big, wide, and mighty river . . . the most significant (and humbling) reminder for me of God's power on my walking route.

Early morning fog on the river, enshrouding the bluffs . . . and making the boats and bridges appear to be floating on clouds.

The old manhole covers with a paddlewheel steamship design.

Down feathers of a startled dove, floating gently

down from an oak tree along the river, like giant snowflakes.

The orange glow of the sky across the river at sunrise.

A multitude of pink and orange clouds arrayed in formation, like a battalion of starships awaiting an order to attack.

A tugboat chugging along on the river, dwarfed by the barges it is pushing, looking like the little boat that could.

The dense canopy of trees crowded along the river bank, soaring above the bluff like a patch of transported jungle from the Amazon.

Quirky, old, brick dependencies and flickering gas lamps that transport me to 19th-century London ... for a block or two I'm an unnamed character passing through a scene in a Charles Dickens novel.

Ramshackle wood and tin buildings . . . harboring stories long forgotten.

Silhouettes of elegant church steeples, glowing warmly in the first light of the day.

A solid, dark blue cloud on the horizon that looks enough like a mountain range to make me pause for a few seconds to reconfirm I'm in Mississippi, not Colorado.

The architectural diversity, design, and craftsmanship of gable windows I walk by.

Town homes that beckon the passerby to pause and imagine family life within those walls 165 years ago – a decade before the war that would so profoundly affect that life.

The beauty of a thousand snow-white Natchez Crepe Myrtle blooms bobbing in the breeze.

The early-morning stillness of the grounds surrounding Rosalie (a beautiful antebellum house with magnificent grounds, on the bluff), where if I gaze intensely enough I think I might see Union officers milling about, perhaps even Grant himself, under the shade of a pecan tree so tall it seems to touch the sky.

Speaking of Rosalie . . . the way the light shimmers, sparkles, and shifts on the rippled glass panes of the large windows as I walk by early in the morning . . . as if hinting, for the briefest of moments, of a secret, magical world inside . . . a portal to enchantment, beckoning me to enter.

In the final block of my walk . . . a tunnel materializes just ahead, formed by a row of crepe myrtle trees, limbs arching overhead to touch the aged brick wall bordering the sidewalk . . . at the other end, I see a fragment of a large antebellum home . . . the gateway to a Southern Narnia? . . . I enter . . .

Simple? Yes. Interesting? Yes. Little? Often. Reflective? Sometimes. Silly? Sometimes. Fanciful? I hope so. And invariably wonderful, and all bounty of the incredible gift of life. So marvel. Gaze. Wonder. Imagine. Free your inner child!

CHAPTER FOUR

WHY ARE WE HERE?

For you created my inmost being; you knit me together in my mother's womb.

I praise you because I am fearfully and wonderfully made; your works are wonderful, I know that full well.

My frame was not hidden from you when I was made in the secret place. When I was woven together in the depths of the earth, your eyes saw my unformed body.

All the days ordained for me were written in your book before one of them came to be.

- Psalm 139:13-16

My walks are a springboard to deeper thought. I have counted my blessings and am in a gratitude frame of mind. I have heightened powers of observation, and I have allowed my inner child to come forth and be fascinated by all manner of things I pass by, natural and man-made. Then I go a level deeper.

It goes something like this. So why I am here, Lord? I'm privileged to be right here, right now, with the blessings you've bestowed on me and my family. What have I done for you? How have I brought glory to your name? You've put me here for a purpose. You've given me talents. How would you have me use those talents? Guide me, show me, help me fulfill the purpose for which you've given me life.

It's essentially a prayer, acknowledging that God has given me talents, asking Him for clarity on His purpose for me, and seeking His guidance in better accomplishing that purpose. Oddly enough, the answers seem to crystallize at these moments during my walks. Why is that? My mind is relaxed and focused. I have an attitude of gratitude for God's blessings. So maybe I am receptive. Maybe I'm listening for His voice. Maybe I'm humble. I don't know for sure. But I do know my "communication channel" with God is at its highest level of tuning in the middle of my walks, along the river.

Scripture tells us if we come near to God, He will come near to us (James 4:8). It also tells us that, as Christians, through the indwelling Holy Spirit, we are given different gifts, to use for the common good (1 Corinthians 12:4-11). Each of us has a spiritual gift. Each of us has one or more other talents. God wants us to use those gifts and talents in ways that help each other and bring glory to Him. Too many of us fail to recognize we have these gifts. Too many of us fail to use the gifts we know we have. An unused gift or talent is like a light kept under a bowl. We need to free our lights and let them shine, for they are divinely given.

For God, who said, "Let light shine out of darkness," made his light shine in our hearts to give us the light of the knowledge of the glory of God in the face of Christ.
- 2 Corinthians 4:6

One of the constant answers I receive is to develop and use the writing abilities God gave me. *Walking with God* is one of the ideas generated during this portion of my walks. It is the first book in what may become a series with the common title *Let Us Meet at the River*.

Another answer is to be a better father and husband. One of my purposes, I have no doubt, is to raise good children and to do more to help other children. The main reason, I think, my wife Nancy and I clicked early on in our dating years ago, and have never wavered in our commitment to each other, is our mutual love of children. For both of us, at least with respect to anything in the earthly realm, children are our strongest love and passion. Everything else is secondary.

Do you ever ask God why you are here? How often? Has He answered? If you haven't asked, do so today. If you have asked but not received a clear answer, keep asking. God will answer. He will nudge you in the right direction. Consider Saul's experience on the road to Damascus. Admittedly, he was hit with the equivalent of a divine lightning bolt rather than a divine nudge. But he listened and acted on God's plan for him. Look at his amazing life and accomplishments from that point forward, as Paul.

You have talents uniquely yours, given to you by God. Don't ever doubt you have special talents. If you are stuck trying to figure out what those talents are, or if you know your talents but have failed to develop and use them, try my little prayer at whatever point during your walk it feels most right. It will hit you. You will know. And I'll bet you began to gain clarity and receive answers and inspiration.

You are a unique creation. *No one else exactly like you has ever existed or ever will.* Think about that. God has given each of us special and unique characteristics and attributes. Paul called them gifts of grace (Ephesians 4:7). Maybe you already know what yours are. If not, communicate with God to discover them. They are within you.

Charles Stanley suggests a good way to pinpoint your spiritual gift(s): ask yourself what motivates you. He gave an example of his mother, who always sent cards of encouragement to people who were sick or struggling. He said she had the gift of mercy. What do you enjoy? What are you good at?

God gave you gifts so you would use them. When your

actions are aligned with your talents, your happiness and productivity will soar – and God will be smiling, because He knows you will use those talents to glorify Him. What a win-win He's created for each of us!

This is to my Father's glory, that you bear much fruit, showing yourselves to be my disciples.

- John 15:8

When you arrive back home, write down an action plan based on the insights you gained during your walk. Not every walk will yield an insight. That's ok. Just write down any thoughts that occurred to you. Soon enough a picture or a plan will emerge.

Then take the most important but most difficult step. Take action! We have to stop procrastinating. "Tomorrow" may be the most destructive word in our vocabulary. We tend to believe that tomorrow always comes and that – until I presume we are in our twilight years – our life here on earth will go on forever (so what's the harm in putting off action until "tomorrow"?). Big mistake! I know. My middle name should be "Procrastination." All we have for sure is today, the present. *Tomorrow is not guaranteed.*

Don't make my frequent mistakes of "waiting until conditions are perfect" and "let me research or study that some more before doing anything." It's far better to get started, make mistakes (which will happen regardless), learn from them, make course corrections, and keep pushing forward. Set deadlines. Banish fear by acting – and by realizing the worst case scenario isn't that bad.

I respect and even envy veterans who've seen combat.

Respect, for their courageous dedication to preserving our freedom and for unflinchingly performing their duties as determined by their commands. You can't reach a higher level of dedication or performance than placing yourself in harm's way and being willing to make the ultimate sacrifice. That subject is worthy of a library of books. I've read a number of them, and each one reinforces my awe and admiration for our hero soldiers.

Envy, because they've faced fear beyond anything most

of us will ever experience, and survived the experience. So how insignificant must the petty fears that hold us back seem to them? I imagine many combat veterans charge full steam ahead, damn the torpedoes. As a result, they accomplish their goals and build successful businesses. I would not be surprised if studies show a higher percentage of entrepreneurship among veterans than the general population.

Relish the moment, and take some action, now. We are not walking through a mine field or driving a Hum-vee into a possible ambush. We are not doing a nighttime HALO jump behind enemy lines. If things go wrong, we won't end up with an arm or leg blown off, shrapnel in the chest, or dead.

Yet fear is the biggest reason we fail to act on great ideas, inspired plans, and divine direction. Fear is real, and it paralyzes us. What are we afraid of? The unknown. Stepping outside our comfort zones, even though those zones are holding us back and making us unhappy. Fear of failure. Even fear of success.

We have to find ways to push past our fears. One way is to put them in perspective. Our fears seem absurd in the context of what our soldiers have faced in combat. For just one example, read *Lone Survivor*, by Marcus Luttrell. His true story, of four SEALs trapped on a mountainside in Afghanistan and attacked by an overwhelming force of 100 or more Taliban fighters, contains the most heart-pounding, condensed, non-stop combat I've ever vicariously experienced. Same for the movie version (profanity warning – SEALs are explicit).

The only way I can see that Marcus survived is that God put a hedge of protection around him. Marcus acknowledges that God protected him. Thousands of bullets and grenade fragments missed him by inches. God guided them away from Marcus. Every time he tumbled or was blown down the steep mountainside, his rifle landed close by, as if carried to him by God. He was blown off two ledges by RPG detonations that should have killed him. The second time he was blown into a spot where he could stay concealed. Whatever he does with the rest of his life, my bet is that it will be something great, and it will glorify God.

43

Another way to push past our fears is by listening to God. What does God tell us?

The same thing He told Joshua when, upon the death of Moses, He commanded Joshua to lead the Israelites into hostile territory – the promised land. Joshua was terrified. There he was, taking the place of Moses, and about to cross the Jordan River and come face to face with mighty armies and fortified cities. He had real fears! Imagine the butterflies in his stomach! Take whatever fears we have and multiply them by 10,000 to visualize what Joshua was experiencing.

Here's what God told Joshua:

Have I not commanded you? Be strong and courageous. Do not be terrified; do not be discouraged, for the Lord your God will be with you wherever you go.

- Joshua 1:9

Joshua listened, had faith in God's promise, and was victorious. We can do the same in our daily battles with fear and uncertainty and with our feelings of inadequacy. God tells us to be strong and push forward.

It's hard to imagine feeling more inadequate than Gideon. According to his own account, his clan was the weakest, and he was the least in his family. Yet God chose Gideon to lead the Israelites in battle against their oppressors, the Midianites. When God had his back, Gideon became a "mighty warrior" (Judges 6:11-16). We too, by knowing God is with us, can vanquish our fears and insecurities and accomplish the great things for which we were created. We can become mighty warriors!

A passage in Psalms paints a perfect picture of Almightly God as our protector:

He will cover you with his feathers, and under his wings you will find refuge; his faithfulness will be your shield and rampart.

You will not fear the terror of the night, nor the arrow that flies by day, nor the pestilence that stalks in the darkness, nor the plague that destroys at midday.

A thousand may fall at your side, ten thousand at your right hand, but it will not come near you.

You will only observe with your eyes and see the punishment of the wicked.

If you make the Most High your dwelling – even the Lord, who is my refuge – then no harm will befall you, no disaster will come near your tent.

For he will command his angels concerning you to guard you in all your ways; they will lift you up in their hands, so that you will not strike your foot against a stone.

You will tread upon the lion and cobra; you will trample the great lion and the serpent.

"Because he loves me," says the Lord, "I will rescue him; I will protect him, for he acknowledges my name.

He will call upon me, and I will answer him; I will be with him in trouble, I will deliver and honor him.

With long life will I satisfy him and show him my salvation."

- Psalm 91: 4-16

Whenever we are scared or insecure, we should read this scripture for powerful, calming reassurance. Why hesitate a moment longer, since we know God is with us? Start today on your new journey!

One small step is enough. Lots of small steps, and big

steps, are great, but just accomplishing one thing is amazing forward progress. As the Chinese proverb says, a journey of a thousand miles begins with a single step. Walk with a mindset of gratitude. Start or continue your thousand-mile journey. Take that step. And keep walking. God is beside you. When you encounter rough passages, just ask Him to carry you through. He will.

So do not fear, for I am with you; do not be dismayed, for I am your God. I will strengthen you and help you; I will uphold you with my righteous right hand.

- Isaiah 41:10

I doubt any of us have faced as much fear as David, who was constantly on the run from King Saul, who wanted to kill him out of jealousy. What did David do? He turned to God, praised Him, and found solace.

I sought the Lord, and he answered me; he delivered me from all my fears.

- Psalm 34:4

47

Use your walks to gain clarity and overcome fear. After all, God put you here to do what He gave you talent to do. He's on your side.

What then, shall we say in response to this? If God is for us, who can be against us? He who did not spare his own Son, but gave him up for us all – how will he not also, along with him, graciously give us all things?

- Romans 8:31-32

I remember using this scripture as a lesson for the 5th graders in my Sunday School class years ago. All of us have bad days, days when it seems the world is against us, when we feel all alone in our struggles, when we've been treated unfairly. Let this scripture be the pick-me-up for you or your child.

What obstacle is too large for God to remove? What burden is too big for Him to lift off your shoulders? What problem is too insurmountable to fix?

There is none. God can move mountains!

What's tugging at your heart or stuck in your mind?

What's your purpose? What are you meant to do, to be, to accomplish? Why *are* you here?

Asking God for clarity and guidance will crystallize the answers, particularly if you are in a mindset of gratitude and your communication channel has eliminated all the static. In a very real sense, my walks are "static eliminators." Try it. And keep trying it.

Whether your channel locks-in the first time or on the 25th walk, it will lock-in. The results go beyond clarity to full-fledged inspiration. Your fears will subside. Your confidence will swell. A sense of peace will flood over you. You'll be happier.

The Bible tells us God will give us the desires of our hearts. But there are some conditions. As you read this book, think about how the daily walks I describe – these "walks with God" – connect with these conditions:

Delight yourself in the Lord and he will give you the desires of your heart. Commit your way to the Lord; trust in him and he will do this:

> *He will make your righteousness shine like the dawn,*
> *the justice of your cause like the noonday sun.*
>
> *Be still before the Lord and wait patiently for him; do*
> *not fret when men succeed in their ways, when they*
> *carry out their wicked schemes.*
>
> *Refrain from anger and turn from wrath; do not fret —*
> *it only leads to evil.*
>
> *For evil men will be cut off, but those who hope in the*
> *Lord will inherit the land.*

- Psalm 37:4-9

What happens when our walks are aligned with God's paths for us . . . when we are *walking with God*?

> *If the Lord delights in a man's way, he makes his steps*
> *firm; though he stumble, he will not fall, for the Lord*
> *upholds him with his hand.*

- Psalm 37:23-24

Wow!

The beneficial effects of clarity of purpose, of aligning your life with the path God has made available to you, will extend into all aspects of your life. But remember, these "energy packets" don't last forever. You need to wind the flywheel back up as often as possible. Daily walks serve that purpose for me.

Distractions, disappointments, our imperfections and lapses, and the countless stresses of daily life all create static. We need to clear the channel and talk with God daily. As your daily walking habit becomes embedded, the channel gets stronger and stays open longer; the static diminishes. It's a compounding effect.

You will begin to notice "divine nudges" that put you and keep you on the path you are meant to follow. Before you realize it, your life has changed. You are impacting others in a more positive way. The force is with you.

You are fulfilling your purpose in life, courtesy of God. Both of you are smiling. Maybe (when no one is looking) you hold hands and skip for a bit, like you and your friends did back in first grade.

CHAPTER FIVE

"GOOD MORNING!"

In reply Jesus said: "A man was going down from Jerusalem to Jericho, when he fell into the hands of robbers. They stripped him of his clothes, beat him and went away, leaving him half dead.

A priest happened to be going down the same road, and when he saw the man, he passed by on the other side. So too, a Levite, when he came to the place and saw him, passed by on the other side.

But a Samaritan, as he traveled, came where the man was; and when he saw him, he took pity on him.

He went to him and bandaged his wounds, pouring on oil and wine. Then he put the man on his own donkey, took him to an inn and took care of him.

The next day he took out two silver coins and gave them to the innkeeper. 'Look after him,' he said, 'and when I return, I will reimburse you for any extra expense you may have.'

Which of these three do you think was a neighbor to the man who fell into the hands of robbers?"

The expert in the law replied, "The one who had mercy on him."

Jesus told him, "Go and do likewise."

- Luke 10:30-37

Is your day hectic? Do you rush to and fro, juggling enumerable tasks? Do the stresses of daily life consume your mental and physical energy? Are you so pulled hither and yonder by external obligations (real or contrived) that you barely notice your neighbor, much less a passing stranger? Is time in such short supply that you don't have any left to think and reflect beyond the next pressing matter on your to-do list? Do you operate mostly on a surface-level, oblivious to the untapped internal forces within you?

Like the priest and the Levite, do you pass by your neighbor, hurriedly and silently? Too complicated or messy to get involved? Too busy trying to handle your own problems? Keep your head down and mouth shut? Focused on your own priorities, and helping a stranger in need isn't one of them?

Welcome to the modern world, the new normal. The speed of life. Alarm goes off, shower, dress, rush kids to school, off to work or store, lunch, more work or to-do matters, pay bills, doctor, soccer, football, meeting, another errand, dinner, cleaning, phone calls, a TV show, homework, kids rounded up and to bed, talk to spouse 15 minutes ("how was your day?" "exhausting." "how was yours?" "same."), go to bed, rinse, repeat, rinse, repeat. Chaotic. Impersonal. Hyper-competitive. Materialistic. Cutthroat. Keeping up with the Joneses. Running with the madding crowd.

But wait. Who says there has to be a new normal? Who makes these rules? Why does everything have to be rushed and superficial? Has a spell been cast on us that makes us act like a hive of busy bees, hamsters on running wheels, an army of angry fire ants, or a horde of caffeine-buzzed zombies? (That last analogy is somewhat paradoxical, but makes for an interesting mental image.)

No. We choose to be that way. We develop habits that become ingrained. We take the path of least resistance. It's easier just to keep with our routines and to fill our minds with busy-body tasks than to slow down (yikes!) and start using the brains and creative powers that God gave us. He's waiting for us to tap the powers. He's probably shaking His head as He watches us scurrying about like mice. "Rat race" is a good way to describe it.

When I get in "rush" mode and start ignoring or being curt with people around me (especially family), and realize it, I think of the song by Simon and Garfunkel, "The 59th Street Bridge Song." (I had to look up the name, because I always call it by its first line.) I also think of Psalm 37:7. Sometimes we need to slow down . . . and even "be still."

God made us to be social. He gave us intelligence to be civilized. He made man in His image. He gave us brains far more complex than any computer ever devised. So why in the world do we so often exhibit anti-social behavior? Why do we so often act like uncivilized barbarians? Or like pre-programmed robots? Why do we only use a small percentage of our brain power? Why do we incessantly rush to the mindless tasks next on our lists instead of pausing for a bit each day to do the deeper thinking of which we are capable?

Many people from other regions of the country make fun of Mississippi (and the South in general). They adopt, propagate, and reinforce the stereotypes. People are fat. They eat too much fried chicken. They are poor. They are uneducated. They talk too slowly. They think too slowly. They are just a bunch of rednecks. They live in clapboard houses and sit around on the porch. Blah, blah, blah.

The people who think and say those things should visit. Their laughter and ridicule would stop. I think their jaws would drop in amazement. There is plenty of culture. Literary, musical, artistic talent abounds. Plenty of successful people live here. A cross-section of the population would be indistinguishable in most respects from the people in any other state. It's true that much of the food is comforting, but it's good (really good!).

Mississippi is as naturally beautiful as any state in America. Intelligence is the same as elsewhere. A marketing person would say all these things are "features." The real selling points, however, are "benefits." This is where Mississippi and the South have a not-so-well-kept secret. One that the rest of America, in this age of the "new normal," could really benefit by adopting.

Nothing is wrong with a fast-paced, activity-filled, success-oriented lifestyle. Our economy thrives on competition. Capitalism and disruption are the catalysts for societal progress. Free-market economies and industrial/technological innovations have done far more to improve the human condition than anything else in the history of mankind.

Children need extra-curricular activities. Juggling lots of stuff at one time is just part of life. Everyone who wakes up, enters the arena, and does his best to provide for his family is to be commended. Even more so the countless number of people who go above and beyond to help others.

I'm talking about an intangible here. Something that will not interfere with your other activities (although it may result in some of them being eliminated or re-prioritized). Something that will actually make your activities more enjoyable and more productive. Something that will make you happier and rub off on those around you. Something that will help you tap into the internal wellsprings of creativity and spirituality that bubble up during your walks.

What's the secret? Just being friendly! Putting a smile on your face and saying "good morning" or "hello" to people you pass on the street or walking path or run into during the day. Saying "thank you." Holding a door open for others. Engaging in small talk. Being genuinely social. Laughing more. Pausing for a moment here and there to really talk to and care about your neighbors, not just exchange perfunctory greetings.

That's it? Try it before you dismiss it as silly or insignificant. Smiling, voicing a greeting, and laughing are big deals. You'll feel happier, and you'll make the other people you interact with happier. Even if it's hard or awkward at first, please stick with it. You soon may have your entire community smiling, greeting each other, and laughing. It's natural down here in the South. People by and large are happy. The pace of life may be a shade slower, but that allows more time for people to talk, and it directly affects happiness. *People* are the most important thing, rather than *things* being the most important thing. The difference in perspective is profound.

I always know when I pass by a tourist along the river bluff. Four out of five times, the tourist will not make eye contact, or if he does, he will not speak. When I say "good morning," I get a stare, startled look, or scowl. I feel like they perceive me as they would an interstellar alien. I've unexpectedly intruded into their defensive force field. I've done something off the radar. The tourist's brain is trying to process the situation in a micro moment. *Is this person a threat? What does he want? What if he stops and talks? What should I do?* A few steps beyond, I invariably smile and shake my head ever so slightly.

People from other regions of the country who have not spent time in the South are often unprepared for how friendly people are down here. It's amusing. But it offers a lesson in human interaction. I have not studied the science, but common sense and observation make it clear enough. People crave being acknowledged. People are social by nature. Smiling is contagious. Laughter reduces stress and rebalances emotions.

People who smile, greet, and laugh – and visit long enough to ask (and genuinely care about) how you're doing and how's Aunt Thelma and did you hear about Joe's illness and by the way congratulations on Johnny's game last night – are happy people. They have the same problems, losses, stresses, and life stuff as everyone else, but they've chosen to be happy as a general rule, day in, day out. They make others happier. When bad things happen, those "others" are there for support and encouragement.

People are so informal in the South, on an everyday basis, even when they try to be more formal it ends up being casually endearing. Instead of addressing an older person by that person's last name (Mr. Smith, Mrs. Jones), they use the first name (Mr. James, Miss Nancy).

I've read that Charleston is the "friendliest city" in America. Many southern towns could vie for the title. It's not a competition, though, and many other communities across the country are full of friendly people. Here in the South it's the essence of the culture, because people and family are at the top of the "most important" list.

People here still want things, of course. And normal human frailties abound. Violence, envy, pettiness, hurtful behavior, immorality, corruption, and all manner of other sins and inequities still flourish. There is poverty. People in the South are more like other people than they are different. They are miles away from perfect. But perfection's not the issue, and no one can achieve it anyway.

It's a matter of perspective and priority. People down here, for the most part, have chosen to savor life by slowing down a bit. They take the time to be friendly. Some may have less, some may be hurting inside, some may have physical pain, but they still portray happiness more often than not. I find it all pretty inspiring. I know if you're around it for any period of time it rubs off on you.

It's related, I think, to the attitude of gratitude discussed earlier. People are happy to be alive, to live in a beautiful town, to be connected with family, to be able to enjoy and appreciate little things. They know where blessings come from. They know they're blessed even in the midst of affliction. They are more optimistic than pessimistic. They have hope.

When you find yourself hurried or anxious, hurting or in need, slow down for a moment. And follow Paul's example:

Rejoice in the Lord always. I will say it again: Rejoice!

Let your gentleness be evident to all. The Lord is near.

Do not be anxious about anything, but in everything, by prayer and petition, with thanksgiving, present your requests to God.

And the peace of God, which transcends all understanding, will guard your hearts and your minds in Christ Jesus.

Finally, brothers, whatever is true, whatever is noble, whatever is right, whatever is pure, whatever is lovely, whatever is admirable – if anything is excellent or praiseworthy – think about such things.

Whatever you have learned or received or heard from me, or seen in me – put it into practice. And the God of peace will be with you.

> *I know what it is to be in need, and I know what it is to have plenty. I have learned the secret of being content in any and every situation, whether well fed or hungry, whether living in plenty or in want.*
>
> *I can do everything through him who gives me strength.*
>
> - Philippians 4:4-9, 12-13

Crossing paths with friendly people who take a second to greet each other is like advancing through a video game in which golden bonus nuggets are always bouncing into your path, allowing you to grab them. Each time you do, you get a "power up" energy boost. If your environment is not yet so friendly, be the one who scatters golden bonus nuggets. If you are walking with God, maybe you'll transform an entire community. At the very least, you'll transform yourself.

Now say it with a smile – "good morning!"

CHAPTER SIX

ACROSS OUR PATHS

Other seed fell among thorns, which grew up and choked the plants. Still other seed fell on good soil, where it produced a crop – a hundred, sixty or thirty times what was sown. He who has ears, let him hear.

- Matthew 13:7-8

The one who received the seed that fell among the thorns is the man who hears the word, but the worries of this life and the deceitfulness of wealth choke it, making it unfruitful.

But the one who received the seed that fell on good soil is the man who hears the word and understands it. He produces a crop, yielding a hundred, sixty or thirty times what was sown.

- Matthew 13:22-23

When you start walking with the mindset described in the preceding chapters – gratefulness, wonderment, reflection, prayer, connection with others – you'll experience a clarity and focus that is incapable of adequate description. You will have removed layers of "protective coatings" that have obstructed introspection.

We build up these layers over time, consciously or unconsciously, actively or passively. Like cataracts on the eyes, they have clouded the mind's ability to move beyond surface-level analysis to a deeper level of assessment and then recalibration based on that understanding.

Picture yourself peeling off layers of an onion's skin. At some point during your walks you'll have stripped away enough to reveal what's hiding inside – you! Who you really are, today. For most of us, that revelation is not entirely pleasing.

We have an ideal vision of who we want to be, who we see ourselves being, what characteristics, qualities, and attributes we want to have. But the picture that emerges doesn't match the vision. Often the two are wildly different.

Use the two images to begin a process of shedding the parts of your "self" – your habits, thoughts, communications, actions, reactions, behaviors, and interactions with family, friends, and others – that don't line up with your ideal vision, so that you are continually moving closer and closer to the ideal.

Don't worry if you don't fully get there, especially if your ideal is near-perfection (being Christlike, for example, as I discuss in a later chapter). It's the movement, the improvement, the awareness and course corrections that will shine through soon enough.

None of us can achieve anything close to perfection. It's good to have a lofty standard or goal, so long as we understand the journey is the thing, and incremental improvements are good – and we don't let failure to reach an ideal discourage us. Each forward step on the journey is positive progress! The important thing is to keep walking. Do-overs, re-sets, stumbles, and switchbacks are all part of walking through the valley and up the mountain.

What if your ideal vision of yourself is fuzzy? In the case

of an under-developed vision, you will discover that your walks will help you crystallize a vision.

One of the most common problems of self I've observed is what I've come to call the disease of "Zero Sum," caused by the "viruses" of Misery and Envy. It's a philosophy governing the behavior of people who are "out of sync."

Since you are reading this book, you probably are not a Zero Sum person (ZSP). But the syndrome is so pervasive in our society, and so destructive, I felt compelled to include a chapter on it. My objective is to raise awareness, and to suggest that, by continuing to shine the light of Christ, we can make a positive difference in the lives of the victims and the perpetrators.

What do I mean by "people who are 'out of sync'"? "Out of sync" in this context means they are not at peace with themselves (with whom they really are, deep down), *and* they feel compelled to denigrate anyone they (irrationally) perceive as a threat, challenge, or irritant to their lifestyles and self-validations. It's essentially a psychological defect. Ultimately, however, I think the root cause is a lack of any true relationship with God and Christ.

So what is Zero Sum? Very simply, the perspective that another person's accomplishment, success, happiness, good personality trait, or other positive attribute, is not tolerable because (in the mind of the ZSP) it negatively impacts the ZSP. As a result, and typically when the ZSP fails to "re-mold" the other person to the ZSP's specifications and behavioral standards, the ZSP feels compelled to eliminate the other person's positive attributes. How? By belittling, slandering, and shunning the person and encouraging others to do so.

Zero Sum is a ridiculously false premise, but a very real philosophy that drives the behavior of many people. How can this be so? Because Zero Sum is the product of two extremely powerful emotions that influence human behavior: Misery and Envy. Together, these two "viruses" create a Frankenstein's monster within the afflicted person.

The old adage, "misery loves company," is true. People who are miserable often can't stand to see someone else happy or successful. A positive person (simply by being herself) constantly reminds the miserable person what she is not. That reminder increases the internal turmoil of the miserable person. It makes her feel better knowing that others are also miserable, especially if she pushes them there. There is a euphoria derived from inflicting pain on someone who exhibits happiness and from making that person (at least temporarily) unhappy or insecure.

Like a laser beam, the happy person illuminates and intensifies the misery of the miserable person. And unfortunately, many miserable people react by going after the happy person by spreading lies, making hurtful comments, exclusion, ridicule, even physical violence.

To make matters worse, Misery is egged on by its cohort-in-crime, Envy. The other person's accomplishments and attributes create envy, often obsessive envy. Those accomplishments and attributes need not be material wealth. More often than not, they are things such as academic success, athletic skills, appearance, self-confidence, good-natured personality, happiness, and a sincerely-Christian lifestyle.

Don't measure your life against someone else's in a

negative way. *Don't live among the thorns.* Be happy for others' successes. Respect their opinions and differences, as they respect yours. Learn from them, be inspired by them. Realize you are a unique creation of God. Strengthen your relationship with Christ so that you can discover – and use – your gifts and talents for your own abundance and the common good. *Scatter your seeds in good soil and watch the blessings multiply!*

A walk with God starts with a single step. God watches over a single sparrow. How much more does He watch over and love us? If our minds and hearts are open, He will reach down and take our hands. He will walk with us.

Life is hard. Tragedies occur. People get sick. People get injured. People die. People get fired. People have wayward children. People have abusive parents or spouses. Marriages fail. The list is endless. Misery is unavoidable in life. The pain is real. No one disputes these things. No one expects you to be Pollyanna in the face of real hurt and suffering.

But we must rethink how we react to the slings and arrows of misfortune. What should we do when times are tough, tragedies occur, and life is beating us down?

First, look to God and trust Him.

What does the Bible say? It doesn't promise a world free from suffering. But God does tell us all things work for good.

> *And we know that in all things God works for the good of those who love him, who have been called according to his purpose.*

> - Romans 8:28

And He is with us, even in the midst of a storm.

> *The Lord Almighty is with us; the God of Jacob is our fortress.*

> - Psalm 46:7

> *I will say of the Lord, "He is my refuge and my fortress, my God, in whom I trust."*

> - Psalm 91:2

And trials and grief forge faith in its purest and most elemental form.

In this you greatly rejoice, though now for a little while you may have had to suffer grief in all kinds of trials.

These have come so that your faith – of greater worth than gold, which perishes even though refined by fire – may be proved genuine and may result in praise, glory and honor when Jesus Christ is revealed.

- 1 Peter 1:6-7

When we feel the deepest pangs of loneliness or despair – when we feel as if the entire world is against us or has abandoned us – we need to pause and remember God has not, and will not, abandon us. Just as Jesus knew He was not alone in the garden of Gethsemane even when all the disciples fled upon His arrest, so we know God is with us.

But a time is coming, and has come, when you will be scattered, each to his own home. You will leave me all alone. Yet I am not alone, for my Father is with me.

- John 16:32

Recognize the pain. Then understand God hears your prayers and will never forsake you. Look to God for strength. Don't be angry with Him or reject Him. God does hear you, and He is with you. (In the next chapter I'll tell you a personal story showing how we learned this truth in the midst of a crisis.)

> . . . *"Never will I leave you; never will I forsake you."*
> - Hebrews 13:5

Seek God as your refuge. Submit to His will. Trust in Him. Use your daily walks to communicate and seek understanding and comfort. You'll develop a peace and inner strength that will help you get through the crisis.

Second, don't seek to inflict your misery onto others.

Guess what? Those "others" can be a source of friendship and support. Why seek to hurt or destroy them? Your loss is not their gain. Their gain is not your loss. God wants us all to have abundance. Those "others" are our neighbors. What does Jesus say about neighbors? He tells us the second greatest commandment is to "love your neighbor as yourself." (Mark

12:31; also see James 2:8, Galations 5:14, Romans 13:9, Luke 10:27, Matthew 19:19, and Leviticus 19:18).

Engage the happy person. Find out why he or she is happy. Odds are you'll find a sympathetic ear and maybe even a new friend. Why be envious? Envy will not increase your wealth, success, accomplishment, or happiness one iota. In fact, it will detract from it, as envy is a negative force that takes up space and effort that could be occupied by and applied to positive forces. Those positive forces include learning and changing – self-improvement.

If your burden is too heavy, ask God for help. He will send others across your path and into your life, to help you share the burden, just as He did for Moses in the wilderness (when Moses felt overwhelmed as God's chosen leader of a multitude of complaining Israelites).

"Where can I get meat for all these people? They keep wailing to me, 'Give us meat to eat!'

I cannot carry all these people by myself; the burden is too heavy for me. If this is how you are going to treat me, put me to death right now – if I have found favor in your eyes – and do not let me face my own ruin."

The Lord said to Moses: "Bring me seventy of Israel's elders who are known to you as leaders and officials among the people. Have them come to the Tent of Meeting, that they may stand there with you.

I will come down and speak with you there, and I will take of the Spirit that is on you and put the Spirit on them. They will help you carry the burden of the people so that you will not have to carry it alone."

- Numbers 11:13-17

Maybe one of those "others" who crosses your path is the person you or someone you know has been unkind toward as a result of misery and envy. Think about that! God sometimes works in mysterious ways, but He does work for your good if you go to Him with a sincere heart.

Why expend energy trying to pull others from higher rungs on their ladders when you could be climbing a ladder yourself? It is not a competition. You can create your own ladder! Where will you find happiness – in a mud pit or on the top of a mountain?

Get rid of all bitterness, rage and anger, brawling and slander, along with every form of malice.

Be kind and compassionate to one another, forgiving each other, just as in Christ God forgave you.

- Ephesians 4:31-32

This all seems like common sense, but emotions and habits are powerful, and once ingrained, hard to change. This is where daily walks can make a difference. Instead of wallowing in misery and envy, we count our blessings, communicate with God, and connect with others in positive ways. Our perspective and outlook change. Our confidence increases. Our emotional inner strength increases. Our physical strength increases. Our worries decrease as we realize God's got it covered.

We begin to see others not as objects of envy or targets to attack with Misery Arrows, but as sources of positive things – support, understanding, friendship, communication, or even just a smile or nod. Instead of criticizing others 80% of the time and complimenting 20%, we should strive to reverse that ratio and then continue to improve from there. (This is a memo to myself!).

Find the good in people and acknowledge it.

Our God of compassion comforts us, so that when the time comes, we can comfort others.

> *Praise be to the God and Father of our Lord Jesus Christ, the Father of compassion and the God of all comfort, who comforts us in all our troubles, so that we can comfort those in any trouble with the comfort we ourselves have received from God.*

- 2 Corinthians 1:3-4

Who knows where it will lead? But rest assured the path will be graced with golden nuggets instead of littered with trash. Remember, we are all children of God. We should all act more like a family. Our lineage is holy. God has extended grace to each of us countless times. Can we not do the same to our neighbors?

> *Be imitators of God, therefore, as dearly loved children and live a life of love, just as Christ loved us and gave himself*

up for us as a fragrant offering and sacrifice to God.
                                              - Ephesians 5:1-2

Instead of Zero Sum, as Christians we should think and practice Infinite Sum, Infinite Kindness, and Infinite Love for others who come across our paths.

CHAPTER SEVEN

GOD IS IN CONTROL

"Are not two sparrows sold for a penny? Yet not one of them will fall to the ground apart from the will of your Father. And even the very hairs of your head are all numbered. So don't be afraid; you are worth more than many sparrows."

- Matthew 10:29-31

Walking in the early morning along a scenic route, before many people are out and about, watching the sun rise, watching the river rolling ever on, watching a lone bird perched on the top of a gazebo, seeing the fog settled in along the bluff and over the water, feeling the chill of the air – all these things make me cognizant of two things – two realities that are a paradox. First, how small each of us is in relation to the magnitude and majesty of God's creation. Second, that He uniquely created each of us, knows and loves us, watches over us, and wants us to fulfill our potential. So small, yet so great!

As I walk in this type of setting, and perceive this paradox of smallness and greatness, I am filled with a feeling of both insight and peace as in my mind I hear God telling me, "I am in control – I hear you." I realize He knows me, my situation, my worries, my fears, my prayers, my aspirations, everything. I also realize He is watching to see if I listen to Him, if I am being still and quiet and listening for His voice, His direction, His guidance, His will.

Knowing God is in control and He hears us does amazing, positive things. It brings a sense of calm and peace in the midst of crisis, pain, and anxiety. It removes the overwhelming burden of having to deal with tough and tragic situations alone or solely on a human level. Our strength and limits of endurance are finite, but God's are infinite.

Come to me, all you who are weary and burdened, and I will give you rest. Take my yoke upon you and learn from me, for I am gentle and humble in heart, and you will find rest for your souls. For my yoke is easy and my burden is light.

- Matthew 11:28-30

We are all too often quick to anger at God when He doesn't snap to our command to intervene immediately and produce a miracle for us or give us things we ask for. We should instead be listening for His voice and His will, and submitting to it humbly, knowing He hears our requests and understands our pain.

We have a deeply personal story that illustrates God is in control, and He does hear us. I hope it will help and inspire you in a time of crisis.

It was 2004. Our oldest son, Joshua, was excited to be going off to college and playing football at Hardin-Simmons University in Abilene, Texas. He had an accomplished high-school career playing wide receiver and defensive back at Wimberley High School, in the Texas

Hill Country close to Austin. He was in top physical shape. That he would be fighting for his life a few weeks later was the last thing we could have imagined.

The third or fourth game of the season was a night game at a nearby college. I did not go, but got an update from my friend Darrell Franklin, who was there watching his son and the team. I recall the phone call like it was yesterday. He told me Josh caught a pass and had taken a really hard hit just after he caught the ball. As I recall, Darrell was surprised that Josh was able to get up.

When we were able to talk to Josh, he told us his hip hurt, he was bruised and sore. The next day he saw the team doctor. The diagnosis was muscle contusion or something similar. I recall Josh calling to tell us that night he had been in the library, and when he tried to get up from his chair, he fell.

I'll let my wife, Nancy, tell the story from here.

I was at a low point in my faith the night Josh got injured. I was hurting inside for my oldest daughter, who was being bullied by other girls in school. Despite my efforts to do everything right by regularly attending church, keeping my daughter active in our church's youth group, and constantly praying for God to bless our family, things got worse for my daughter and better for the other girls.

I recall talking to God just hours before I found out about Josh. Honestly, it was more like lecturing God. I told Him, with bitter sarcasm, what I thought about how He gave out blessings and how well my prayers had worked. I ended that "conversation" by questioning His existence.

I left for Abilene to check on Josh. I didn't pray.

When I saw Josh that evening, I knew he was really sick, that something was really wrong. I took him to the emergency room of the hospital. The ER doctor dismissed Josh's condition as a "stomach bug." I pleaded desperately with the doctor to admit Josh to the hospital, telling him I knew something was seriously wrong. The doctor turned a deaf ear and dismissed Josh. I struggled all night to tend to Josh. His condition worsened.

Early the next morning James called the head football

coach and the team doctor. They got Josh into the hospital. James drove to Abilene with our other four children. The doctor started an IV and antibiotics. I had a thought that I should pray, but I stopped myself. I told myself, *I'm not going to pray, I don't do that anymore.*

We found out the nurse in charge of Josh had gotten sick and gone home, and she forgot to leave medicine instructions with anyone else. As a result, Josh did not receive his second and third doses of antibiotics. Our family doctor already suspected a serious staph infection. Strong antibiotics were the only hope of stopping it.

Our strapping, 190-pound athlete was withering away. Specialists were called in. The infectious-disease doctor confirmed Josh had a raging staph infection in his muscle – at the hip where he had been hit in the game. The muscle had been torn from the bone. He had an abrasion on his arm. The staph apparently gained entry there and immediately migrated to the spot of the injury, where the bacteria began a feeding frenzy. Josh's body was being flooded with the invading bacteria. The infection had entered the bloodstream. Sepsis was setting in.

The doctors prescribed a potent mix of antibiotics, a cocktail so strong it had to be specially ordered. They flooded Josh's body with antibiotics to fight the rapidly-spreading infection. A war was raging within Josh's body. His immune system was being overwhelmed. His organs and vital systems were at risk of shutting down.

Since the infection was so strong and had been building and multiplying for several days before the first dose of antibiotics, the doctors could not provide any reassurance to us that Josh would be ok.

Josh was moved to the heart-patient floor after the mishap with the initial antibiotic doses. He began having trouble breathing. His oxygen level was dangerously declining. The doctors moved him into the ICU. Josh's condition continued to worsen.

I began praying unceasingly. I knew at that point God was the only one who would be able to help. Everything began to blur. All I recall is praying all the time and feeling like I was neglecting our two youngest children, not feeding or bathing them. My family was camped out in the waiting area, with little food or sleep.

I stayed in the chapel. I read scriptures, silently and out loud. I prayed on my knees. I felt like God was telling me to prepare for Josh's death. I prayed more.

Josh was getting worse.

Suddenly I felt nothing.

My heart became cold to God. I felt all alone.

I thought, *God's not with me, He's turned away from me because of the things I've said and thought about Him.*

It was Sunday morning. I remember walking out of the chapel into the waiting room. I was empty inside. My son was dying.

I dragged myself to a chair. My head was down, but not in prayer. But I did speak to God.

This is what I said:

God, you don't hear me. You've left me. I don't feel your presence. I don't feel like you're going to be in my life anymore. Have you just shut me off?

I had never felt so alone and helpless.

I glanced up and noticed a pretty, well-dressed woman approaching. I immediately thought she was with Child Protective Services – someone must have told her we've had our young children up here for days.

The woman walked over to me. I tried to avoid eye contact. She asked me if I was the mother of the boy in the ICU, the football player. I told her I was.

This is what she said:

I don't know if this is going to make any sense to you, and I've never done anything like this before, but I was sitting in Sunday School, and God put it on my heart that I needed to come see you and give you a message. Everyone told me not to go, not to give you false hope and not to say anything.

She hesitated a moment, and then said:

God hears your prayers. He is listening.

Tears streamed down my face. I was unable to speak.

I knew at that moment, the moment I heard her message, God was real, and He wanted me to surrender all to Him.

I immediately thought, *This woman had answered the exact question I had asked God! And it was God's message to me . . . to me, personally!*

I walked with this woman, this messenger of God's, into the chapel. I kneeled at the alter and prayed with my three girls. The woman began playing a beautiful song on the piano, and singing.

I continued to pray at the altar, my tears still flowing. This is what I prayed:

God, you know my heart . . . you know my heart. Josh is yours. He's always been yours. You've allowed me to parent him. You know best. I surrender all to you, God. Your will be done.

Surrendering my son to God was the hardest thing I've ever done. I might never see my son again until I was in Heaven. I knew now Josh may not live, but that God knew best.

When the woman finished the song, we hugged, and I thanked her for coming to see me and deliver God's message. A profound sense of peace came over me. I was filled with gratitude that God loved me so much that He would send a personal message to me.

The woman who delivered God's message told me she was the wife of Josh's nurse (Josh's main nurse was a man). I have no recollection of her name. [If she reads this story some day . . . thank you for what you did!] She said her husband had told her about Josh and his family. She also said she had never visited any patient of her husband's, in 16 years of his caring for patients at the hospital. But God's voice was so strong and undeniable, she said she could not ignore it.

I left the chapel. I wanted to see Josh. I needed to say goodbye, if that was God's will. Josh was unconscious in the ICU. I had to wait to get in to see him because access was strictly limited. I had been waiting about 30 minutes to go back when the nurses came hurrying out, telling us:

Josh is awake. His vital signs are improving. He's taken a turn for the better.

A miracle was occurring before our very eyes! The doctors could not explain Josh's dramatic turnaround. One of them said he'd never seen anything like it. But we knew. God was healing Josh!

The next day Josh was moved out of the ICU. He continued to strengthen. The infection was receding. He stayed in the hospital another week. He had dropped from 190 pounds to 140 and was in a wheel chair. But he was alive! He continued to get better and gain weight over the balance of the year.

Looking back, I see I was going through the motions with God regarding my daughter and her troubles from other girls in school. We were going to church, doing bible studies. I had my daughters in the church youth group. I had the boxes checked. But I was still doing what I wanted to do. I still got angry and envious. I wasn't close to God, in my heart.

It took a crisis with our son for me to see how real God is and understand that He does hear us, He is listening – and that we need to simply stop and realize how greatly He has blessed us. He gave me an incredible family. We had our health. When Josh lost his health and nearly died, I realized God gives us just what we need at the time. He is in control. I know God listens and loves us. I know I need to listen to Him and submit to His will. God's blessings are amazing!

Back to James:

Nancy's final prayer, just before Josh's dramatic recovery, was in essence the same one Jesus prayed to God in the garden of Gethsemane. Jesus didn't want to die, but He submitted to the Father's will.

> *He went away a second time and prayed, "My Father, if it is not possible for this cup to be taken away unless I drink it, may your will be done."*
>
> - Matthew 26:42

Josh recovered fully. He got married in 2009. He and Erin welcomed a healthy baby boy, Major Murphy Wallace, into the world on January 2, 2015. We just found out Major will be a big brother next year.

Josh's life reminds us, every day, of God's blessings. His life is a testament, for us, of the power of prayer, and a guidepost for how God wants us to pray.

This story is the most powerful one I have to show you God hears our prayers. Nancy and I have a hard time telling this story without choking up, even over a decade later. We are in awe of God's power, grace, mercy, and love. We know Josh is alive only because God healed him. He heard Nancy's prayers and told her so through a wonderful messenger!

God is listening. What are you telling Him? Are you angry, as Nancy was? Are you insisting on giving Him the instructions, insisting He show He is a good and merciful God by doing what you want, right now? Or are you going to God humbly, submitting wholly to His will, acknowledging He is in control, giving Him the glory, whatever the outcome?

This is the confidence we have in approaching God: that if we ask anything according to his will, he hears us. And if we know that he hears us — whatever we ask — we know that we have what we asked of him.

- 1 John 5:14-15

Please read those two verses again, slowly. Now read them once more, pausing to absorb the incredible message. Write the verses on a piece of paper and keep them in your purse or wallet or on your refrigerator or laptop.

Here's the key to walking with God in prayer: "if we ask anything *according to his will*, he hears us."

Think about this when you're walking. Your mindset of gratitude, your open channel of communication, your stillness, introspection, and reflection — all these will have helped you be in a place that can help you release any anger, stop telling God what to do, and deeply and humbly ask for His mercy, forgiveness, and grace, while acknowledging only He is in control . . . and you fully and unconditionally accept His will and His divine power.

However God handles your crisis, you will know He

does hear you, He knows your heart, and all things work for good according to His plan. That's amazing. That's a miracle!

I hope knowing the miracle God bestowed on my family will encourage you to keep the faith and give you comfort in times of pain.

God hears you. Keep praying. He is in control.

CHAPTER EIGHT

REFLECTING THE LIGHT OF CHRIST

I have come into the world as a light, so that no one who believes in me should stay in darkness.

- John 12:46

During the last third of my walks, as a result of the reflections I've made during the first two-thirds – being grateful for another day of life, a happy, well, and safe family, acknowledging all the blessings God has given me, communicating with God and praying about His plan and purpose for my life, how I can use my talents as He wishes, slowing down to enjoy the little things, the moments, smiling and being friendly, being happy for others' successes, and understanding the profound truth that God does hear us and is always in control – I began to contemplate how my actions reflect or don't reflect the light of Christ.

> *"You are the light of the world. A city on a hill cannot be hidden. Neither do people light a lamp and put it under a bowl.*
>
> *Instead they put it on its stand, and it gives light to everyone in the house.*
>
> *In the same way, let your light shine before men, that they may see your good deeds and praise your Father in heaven."*

- Matthew 5:14-16

Am I a beacon that draws people in, or a flickering or failing light that has no positive impact or even pushes people away? Can anyone really tell I am a Christian? Given all the positives flowing from the reflections and realizations generated during my walks, am I walking the talk or just talking the walk? Does the spiritual energy created during my walks translate into positive changes throughout the day and week, or does it simply evaporate as old habits resurface and daily life gets in the way?

The translation of spiritual energy into active changes in how we conduct our lives, how we interact with family, friends, acquaintances, and strangers, and how we are viewed by others, is not easy. The euphoria and excitement built up during the walk began to fade as the real world intrudes and habits go on autopilot. I'm still working to improve my own "energy conversion."

The key, I think, is to keep the perceptions, insights, and motivations generated during the walk front and center throughout the day. Write down the thoughts formed during your walk and the changes promised to yourself – very soon after the walk is finished.

Try using an index card for each walk. Soon you'll have a stack of them, each perhaps with a unique insight, change, promise, goal, or reflection that makes a positive difference in your life and the lives of loved ones. Or try a journal, physical or digital. I kept a "walking log" on my laptop. Now I'm using a composition notebook. Or try sharing the spiritual nuggets with your spouse or family or best friend, so you have an "accountability" partner.

Find ways to capture the energy before it dissipates. Find ways to convert it into action. This same issue arises with respect to mental and creative energy and ideas generated during the walks. Planning and ideas are great, but unless they are converted into action they are wasted. Don't let that happen. Bottle the energy and release it during your daily living, put it into action! (This is another memo to myself!)

Writing and publishing this book were two of the most important action items generated by my walks. Each time I set aside the manuscript, I was soon drawn back to it. "Divine nudges" kept tapping on me to finish it and share this message.

The more we get into this "energy conversion" habit, the more this process will replace old and bad habits, and the easier it will become to maintain the momentum and realize positive changes. Don't be discouraged if you, as I too often do, fail to capitalize on the spiritual energy generated during the walks.

Remember, you rewind the energy flywheel every morning you step out and begin your next walk. Every morning is a reset. Eventually the energy machine will contain so much power, enthusiasm, and revelations that it can't be suppressed. Energy generated is meant to be used!

For this reason I remind you to fan into flame the gift of God, which is in you through the laying on of my hands. For God did not give us a spirit of timidity, but a spirit of power, of love and of self-discipline.

- 2 Timothy 1:6-7

I began to think, during the last part of my walks, of the ways, specifically, I am falling short of being Christlike, of reflecting the light of Christ as an example to others.

Do others see in me a changed person, someone who truly is at peace with the world – with no envy, slow to anger, without an ulterior agenda – someone who seeks to help others, someone who is still, someone who practices what he preaches?

Or do they see something less favorable? Someone who says the right things or advises others how to act, but who frequently and hypocritically doesn't walk his talk?

My goal is to be, sincerely, a "child of light."

For you were once darkness, but now you are light in the Lord. Live as children of light (for the fruit of the light consists in all goodness, righteousness and truth) and find out what pleases the Lord.

- Ephesians 5:8-10

My walks are the best way I've found to redirect my focus on what really matters in life. Over time, they do result in action. Maybe not across the board, but in one or several instances. And those add up to more and more instances.

A change in one area one day and another area another day (or more change in the first area) adds up to a lot of changes. Perfection is not the goal. Two steps forward, one back, two ahead, one back, is still moving in the right direction. None of can be a clone of Christ. We are human, prone to sin, with faults and frailties.

The best we can strive for is to be "Christlike." What does that mean? It means following Christ's teachings and the example of how He lived, consciously, daily, with a sincere heart and committed mind. Sure, we will fall short. We will mess up. That's guaranteed to happen! We will need to seek forgiveness. We will need to apologize. We will say or do the wrong thing. We will hurt loved ones or friends or strangers with our words. We will turn a blind eye to someone in need.

But how much less so will we do all those things if we are consciously striving to be Christlike and using the spiritual energy generated during our walks as fuel to burn that light? It's far better to try, to fail and get up, to keep trying, than to say or think it's too hard so why bother, or to have the attitude that I'll do what I can as long as it's not inconvenient.

It's far better to persevere in your journey to be Christlike than to be a "Sunday Christian." What's a Sunday Christian?

A person who makes an appearance in church, but then doesn't apply one lesson or make one sacrifice or change. Instead, the person goes on with the same self-serving, bad habits the rest of the week, just as though Sunday had never happened. But the person feels good. Everyone saw her in church. She carries herself with an air of piety. Not much different from the Pharisees, really. We don't want to be Pharisees!

Consider what James says:

Do not merely listen to the word, and so deceive yourselves. Do what it says.

Anyone who listens to the word but does not do what it says is like a man who looks at his face in a mirror and, after looking at himself, goes away and immediately forgets what he looks like.

But the man who looks intently into the perfect law that gives freedom, and continues to do this, not forgetting what he has heard, but doing it – he will be blessed in what he does.

- James 1:22-25

The person who listens to, but then ignores scriptural teachings and precepts, is spiritually hollow. He has a body, but no substantive identity. From a Christian perspective, he is an invisible man. Unless he changes, he will pass through life without making any positive or lasting impact on others. He will have blown his opportunity to glorify God by using his God-given spiritual and other talents – talents God wanted him to use! A wasted life. So lacking in impact he even forgets his own face.

In contrast, a doer of the word – a person who hears, believes, and sincerely follows and acts on scripture's divine instructions, made perfect through Christ – finds purpose and fulfillment. That person makes a positive and lasting impact. That person uses the talents breathed into him or her to bring abundance and blessings to others . . . and to himself or herself.

What a difference between just talking the walk and truly walking the talk!

Be an Action Person, not an Invisible Person!

As Paul told the members of the church in Corinth,

sincere, committed Christians are letters from Christ, to the world:

> *You show that you are a letter from Christ, the result of our ministry, written not with ink but with the Spirit of the living God, not on tablets of stone but on tablets of human hearts.*

> - 2 Corinthians 3:3

That's a powerful metaphor when you think about it. I would go a step further and say that Christians striving to be Christlike are love letters to others who don't have Christ in their hearts. Some of those others will respond by accepting Christ and changing their lives! To combine the metaphors of light and letters, we can say that when we are at our best in terms of representing Christ to the world, we are illuminated love letters, attracting others by our glow.

For many of us it's a constant struggle to be Christlike, and a great responsibility, but the rewards are even greater. Be excited you're trying to change. Be excited you've found a way to generate positive energy. Be excited you're working on ways to tap into and use that energy to shine your light.

Be excited you've created a road map! Whether you use the fuel to drive one mile or a hundred today, be excited you're driving in the right direction. You'll start to notice the change, and so will others around you.

You will encounter resistance and criticism. You will upset the equilibrium. Family, friends, and acquaintances who are comfortable living "in and of the world," without any true spiritual ballast, will likely react negatively.

People who've grown accustom to darkness don't like the sudden illumination of a light. The light hurts their eyes. It exposes them. Not through some judgmental "light beam of self-righteousness," but simply because there's a new light, reflecting goodness and purity and love. By its inherent nature it's going to shine on everything around it.

But guess what? If you keep your flame burning, others will begin to react to it in a different way. They will begin to be influenced by your light, your change, your positive, Christlike attributes, behaviors, and actions. Stay the course! The rewards far outweigh the discomfort from the criticisms and judgments of others.

Let's turn again to James for guidance:

My dear brothers, take note of this: Everyone should be quick to listen, slow to speak, and slow to become angry, for man's anger does not bring about the righteous life that God desires.

Therefore, get rid of all moral filth and the evil that is so prevalent and humbly accept the word planted in you, which can save you.

- James 1:19-21

Your light will spark lights within others or cause their flickering or failing lights to burn stronger and brighter. They will want what you have. Eventually, their lights will bolster your light. At times when your flame flickers or wanes, they will be there to fan it. Over time, the power of your lone light will be multiplied a hundred fold!

And everyone who has left houses or brothers or sisters or father or mother or children or fields for my sake will receive a hundred times as much and will inherit eternal life.

- Matthew 19:29

The changes you make, fueled by the spiritual energy from your walks, will bring blessings into your life. The changes in others, encouraged and sparked by your light, can create a thousand points of light. Those thousand points of light can create a million lights. What a difference you'll have made in your life and many other lives!

CHAPTER NINE

RENEWAL

At one time we too were foolish, disobedient, deceived and enslaved by all kinds of passions and pleasures. We lived in malice and envy, being hated and hating one another.

But when the kindness and love of God our Savior appeared, he saved us, not because of righteous things we had done, but because of his mercy.

He saved us through the washing of rebirth and renewal by the Holy Spirit, whom he poured out on us generously through Jesus Christ our Savior, so that, having been justified by his grace, we might become heirs having the hope of eternal life.

This is a trustworthy saying. And I want you to stress these things, so that those who have trusted in God may

be careful to devote themselves to doing what is good.
These things are excellent and profitable for everyone.

- Titus 3:3-8

A big benefit from my walks is a real sense of renewal. Spiritual renewal is the first result. But the positive energy extends to the emotional, mental and creative realms as well. The spiritual calmness and insights that manifest during the walks directly affect my emotional state. This result is probably similar to what those of you who do meditative exercises experience – calmness, rebalancing, letting go of little irksome things, appreciating my family, releasing any anger, and resolving to listen and understand more and to talk and tell less.

At the end of my walks I'm in a mindset that is favorable to forgetting about things others have done that were hurtful to me or my family. And things that cause me to worry. Or lose sleep. Or stress out. The ability to let go of resentment, anger, bitterness, and a "get even" mentality is especially powerful as a healing force. Blood pressure, risk of heart attack, emotional distress, and mental obfuscation all go down.

Toward the end of my walks, I have the feeling of being washed by a spring rain. The baggage and bad stuff are all washed away. A "new" person is blooming.

Little things, even big things, don't matter as much. That argument with a spouse or child now seems silly. The bad attitude of a sales clerk – who cares? All the news headlines and stories about the bad economy, overreaching and out-of-control government, Islamic terrorism, crime, and a dozen other things, all take a back seat to the feeling of renewal and sense of personal empowerment.

The sheer gratitude derived from knowing you've delved well beyond surface-level thoughts to realizations about your spiritual life and your relationships and have a plan (even if it's just doing one thing better or differently) that you still have time to put into action – is itself a mighty emotion that will carry you forward.

That's the neat thing – the anticipation of the actions

you're going to take, the changes you're going to make, and the things you're going to say to loved ones – as a result of the energy packets you created during your walk. It's almost like the anticipation that builds up during the Christmas season as children gaze at their presents and count down to Christmas day.

This sense of renewal gets back to regaining the wonderment of a child. It really is almost childlike excitement. You've realized how blessed you are. You've been still. You've marveled at the world God created – the big things and the small things. You've listened for His voice. You know He is listening to yours. You've thought about why you are here, your purpose in life. You've reconnected with happy. You've released envy. Instead of dragging others down, you've realized they may help you – and that God is in control. Your light is shining brighter. All of a sudden, you get a feeling that you're a new you, cleansed, purified, simplified, stripped of negative baggage, focused, and grateful to have another day to make a positive difference. You feel renewed, like a "new construction." You have bundled energy ready to release!

The great thing about walking daily is that you can experience this renewal every day. If you slip or waste the energy from yesterday's walk, no big deal. You will recharge the battery, rewind the flywheel today. Every day can be a renewal – whether it recreates or adds onto what was accomplished on yesterday's walk. It's that easy. It's not the Olympics, where years of training come down to one performance.

The daily practice of walking and creating spiritual, emotional, and mental energy packets is both embryonic and accretive. It can be created from scratch, every day. And it can transform you over time into the exact person God created you to be by building on the positive changes and actions previously made and taken.

When your mind is renewed, you are fine-tuned to God's channel for communicating with you and discovering His will for your life.

Do not conform any longer to the pattern of this world, but be transformed by the renewing of your mind. Then you will be able to test and approve what God's will is – his good, pleasing and perfect will.

- Romans 12:2

It is amazing how a simple walk can be the catalyst to transform an under-performing, off-track, confused, unhappy, unpleasant, and/or unfulfilled life into one that fully uses God-given talents, makes a difference, leaves a legacy, and becomes a beacon of light that inspires others. It is amazing that simple walks can get us out of a rut and into the arena of life.

To paraphrase a well-known saying, instead of dying with the profound regret of what could have been, you beautifully run the bases of life and slide into homeplate, dusty, battered, and worn out, and are greeted by God telling you with a smile, "Well done, my good and faithful servant – *well done.*"

Wow! How cool would that be? Just picture it. It can be!

CHAPTER TEN

CREATIVE ENERGY

For the eyes of the Lord range throughout the earth to strengthen those whose hearts are fully committed to him.

- 2 Chronicles 16:9

For we are God's workmanship, created in Christ Jesus to do good works, which God prepared in advance for us to do.

- Ephesians 2:10

A bonus benefit emerges from the process of walking and thought described in earlier chapters. The spiritual and emotional clarity come first. But then comes a mental clarity. The excess baggage and distractions are gone. Suddenly, you are light of foot, clear of mind, and almost floating. I sometimes picture myself running along the surf line on a beach. It's almost as if heavy leg weights have been removed. Or as if I'm suddenly on the moon, with only 1/6 of the gravity of the earth. I'm bounding along.

Creative energy! My mind is focused. Do you want to become an idea machine, as James Altucher encourages? Start walking! Ideas sometimes seem to come by the minute. Other times they pop into my head more slowly, but as often as not I get at least one new creative thought. Sometimes I get new insights or action-items for existing ideas that were already percolating.

The key thing is that the environment is conducive to the generation of ideas. Be ready for them. Remember them so you can write them down, or record a memo on your cell phone, or scribble a note on a small memo pad that you carry with you.

Not every walk yields a brilliant idea or creative thought. Sometimes – particularly if I've skipped walking for a day (or two or three) – it's a big goose egg. No idea. Nothing. But here's the thing: it's ok. On my "goose-egg" days I have learned to simply enjoy the moment. I listen to the songs of the morning birds. I watch the river rolling on. I feel the breeze on my face. I savor life in the present, the right here, right now. That's a reward in itself!

Are you artistic? Or do you want to be? Do you have latent talent? The landscapes, people, macro scenes, images – all seem to pop out to be noticed. As if they know you're looking and open to them.

Sunrises, early-morning fog, quirky and skewed mixes of rooftops, tugboats, the Mississippi River bridge, the bluffs, the churches and their steeples and towers, a person who passes by, an animal, even a weird-looking plant – everything presents itself as a willing subject to make up a story about.

Often I'll make up a short story based on the most intriguing thing I see on my walk. At some point I'll have enough stories to fill a book with a story for each day of the year. Occasionally a short story keeps going, until I find myself working on a potential book. The habit of walking, observing, creating a story, and then writing it down fuels the imagination and the practice of writing every day.

If you paint or draw or sculpt, watch for subjects as you walk. My guess is that you'll have a half-dozen from which to choose after your walk is finished. A lone cardinal atop a tree? A mysterious person you haven't seen before? A church steeple at sunrise? A curious squirrel? Flowers blooming? The hazy outline of trees in the fog?

Are you a photographer – novice or expert? Take your camera on these walks! I've captured some pretty cool pictures just with my iPhone, as a total amateur. Our local newspaper has published a half-dozen of them, for all to enjoy.

Are you an entrepreneur? Or want to be? Try walking! The ideas often come fast and furious once you're in the zone. When you get home, write them down. One may be pure gold. Or none. But soon you'll have dozens of ideas captured. Soon enough, one or two of those will be really good. These walks generate mental and creative energy, just as they do spiritual energy, just as they create emotional balance.

Take advantage of these energy packets after your walk. If you, like me, get off track in your walking schedule – miss several days or more – you'll appreciate even more the mind/ideas renewal and regeneration you get from the walks, because you'll probably notice a little stagnation (as I do). The walks keep my mind fresh, engaged, stimulated, and focused. They keep it generating and percolating ideas, stories, plans, and improvements, and wind it up for taking action.

Are you curious about the world around you? About history? Science? How things work? It's amazing how many things we notice when we are looking. And how we miss so many things all around us when we are too rushed or distracted by life's daily tasks and problems.

What's the history behind that antebellum house I walk by every morning? Or that one? Who were their first owners? What did they do? Where was the elaborate fountain at Memorial Park crafted? What year?

How do those little tugboats push all those barges? I saw one pushing 32 barges! What kind of engines do they have? How much horsepower? How do they turn fast enough to avoid the shallow spots that Mark Twain wrote about in *Life on the Mississippi*? That book, by the way, makes the job of steamboat pilot seem impossible. They had to memorize every mile of the river and know exactly where to navigate day or night. I wonder how things have changed since then, as the memory, fortitude, and skill required, as Twain described it, seem beyond the reach of mere mortals. It made me nervous just reading about it.

How did the artisans and craftsman of the day create such magnificent, detailed buildings, with all the carvings, decorative facades, and complex engineering? St. Mary's Cathedral, built in 1842-43, is a marvel of aesthetic and structural ingenuity and craftsmanship. So is Longwood, the 32-room, 30,000 square-foot, octagonal, Oriental Revival home of Dr. Haller Nutt, with its magnificent rotunda and innovative design. The workmen dropped their tools at the outbreak of the Civil War, with only the first floor (the basement) finished. The upper five floors depict a moment frozen in time.

What Union troops occupied Rosalie? Is there a book or article that tells about their daily life, their interaction with the citizens of the town? Grant stayed at Rosalie (his writing desk is still there). How long was he in Natchez?

How is King's Tavern still standing, being constructed mostly of wood? It was built in the 1700s. Speaking of King's Tavern, what's the full story on the skeleton someone found in the wall, with a dagger in it? Look that up. And read the ghost stories – Madeline the mistress, and the crying baby.

How did the steam engines work on the paddlewheel boats that plied the waters of the Mississippi? Why were they so dangerous? What happened in the 1866 steamboat accident that claimed the life of John McMurran, attorney, planter, and original owner of the antebellum mansion and estate known as Melrose?

What are the biggest fish in the Mississippi River? Catfish? Gar? How big are they? Could they pull a man underwater? How dangerous are the currents and undertows? How cool (and maybe scary) would it be to kayak from the headwaters of the Mississippi to the Gulf? Has anyone done that and written a book about the journey and experiences?

How old is that brick in that wall? Who put it there? How did they make all those bricks? What were their lives like? What would it have been like to have lived in the world of William Johnson, the freed slave turned successful businessman, known as the barber of Natchez, back in the 1830s? My walks take me right by his house (now a museum and part of the Natchez National Historical Park).

The list of questions, topics to explore, things to learn, is endless. If you want to stretch your mind, keep your brain cells active and stimulated, start walking and observing. See what catches your eye and your imagination. It's fun!

If you research just one thing you notice during your daily walk, even if you miss some days, you'll have learned 300 or more things in one year. Your family and friends will think you're a genius or scholar, or a scholarly genius.

And you'll never run out of topics to captivate your friends at parties. When they ask how you know so much, you can just smile and feign modesty, while inwardly you glow from the accolades. All from walking, observing, and following up – using and applying the mental energy you generate during your walk.

Walk daily. Walk thoughtfully. Walk spiritually. Walk with stillness and focus. Walk for emotional rebalancing. Walk for mental and creative energy. Apply your insights, reflections, resolutions, and ideas to change your life in positive ways. Do this faithfully, and who knows what could happen.

You may become a modern-day Leonardo da Vinci. Or your own, unique shining light – the person God created you to be, full of talent and potential and ready, willing, and able to use that talent to achieve amazing things. And you will have within you the direction and power to make a difference. And what a difference that can be!

CHAPTER ELEVEN

MAKE A DIFFERENCE

I became a servant of this gospel by the gift of God's grace given me through the working of his power.

Although I am less than the least of all God's people, this grace was given me: to preach to the Gentiles the unsearchable riches of Christ, and to make plain to everyone the administration of this mystery, which for ages past was kept hidden in God, who created all things.

His intent was that now, through the church, the manifold wisdom of God should be made known to the rulers and authorities in the heavenly realms, according to his eternal purpose which he accomplished in Christ Jesus our Lord.

In him and through faith in him we may approach God with freedom and confidence.

- Ephesians 3:7-12

The daily walks, as I mentioned, make me realize how small and fleeting one person is in the scheme and timeline of the world and the universe, but also how unique and special each person is, in God's eyes. These realities make me want to have some lasting impact, some lasting legacy that will live on. They make me want to make a difference. I bet they do you, too, when you stop to ponder it.

If you don't make a difference, what's the point? You were born, you lived, did some stuff, and died. Gone forever, never to return to the world. Whatever you did while you walked on the earth is all you'll ever do as a human. Whatever that was will be your legacy. What will it be? Nothing, really? Or something enduring? Something that will positively impact others long after you've breathed your last?

Children are our greatest legacies. Parent wisely. Parent lovingly. Parent so that your legacies will live their own lives well, successfully, lovingly, and wisely. Make sure your light is shining on your children first, while they are still young. Don't set yourself up for regrets after they're grown and gone. Your children will reflect and carry on whatever you've taught them (primarily by example, not lecture), for better or worse. Make it better!

Our next legacies are things we create. Our writings, art, music, photographs, and other tangible works of creation that will be read, admired, listened to, looked at, and maybe even discussed, interpreted, and learned from. Works of intellect, works of passion. Works that inspire others to create. Works that inspire others to improve their lives. Works that make people laugh or cry. Works we can each create by using the minds and talents we were given.

Whether on a grand scale or micro scale, works we create now will live on after we are gone. They may affect one person, a hundred, several thousand, or even millions. So get to work making a difference, leaving a legacy, creating tangible works that add value to the world. What gift did God grace you with? Don't let feelings of unworthiness or inadequacy stop you. They didn't stop Paul. He called himself "less than the least of all God's people." Yet consider what he accomplished!

You say you're not an artist or writer? You're not a creative person? Are you an entrepreneur, or are you good at your work? Your company or your work is one of your legacies. And that work need not be "for profit." You could be a volunteer for one or more charitable causes. Do you think Mother Teresa left a legacy that has impacted others? You could be a great mom or dad. Your children are the best legacies. Whether in the business world, charitable world, or family world, you are – or could be – creating tangible value and intangible value.

Look at what Frank McKinney has done (and continues to do), from modest beginnings. He started out as a tennis coach. Now he builds multi-million-dollar mega mansions on speculation. He has used his wealth to build entire villages in Haiti. He is still doing so, and he has inspired many others to join him. Read his wonderful book, *The Tap*, where he reveals his journey to spiritual fulfillment and powerfully explains how each of us should be aware of, and ready to act on, God's taps – those special moments when God presents us with unique opportunities to make a difference and is tapping on our shoulders to nudge us into action.

When we are ready for God's tap, He will tap us. But He doesn't stop there. As Patrick Wood points out in his insightful article entitled "Co-Laboring with God" (published in 2012 by InTouch Ministries® in its magazine), when we are filled with the Holy Spirit and our hearts are receptive, God will breathe His creativity and inspiration into us – just as He did with Solomon, Noah, Joseph, and others in biblical times. Wow! That's incredible.

Wood tells the story of Randall Wallace as just one modern-day example of this truth. Wallace, then an unknown screenwriter, found himself suddenly out of a job due to a writer's strike. He fell to his knees and prayed. He submitted the future of his work to God's will, regardless of the impact on his family. Wood relates that Wallace felt a surge of humility and courage . . . and then words began forming in his mind. Those words were the beginnings of *Braveheart.* The success of that movie launched Wallace's career. Wallace has gone on to produce an acclaimed body of work that acknowledges God's greatness.

Can we really experience the same divine inspiration and intervention? Yes. All we have to do is ask! Wood closes his article with two scripture passages. Ponder them, and marvel at the simplicity.

Call to me and I will answer you and tell you great and unsearchable things you do not know.

- Jeremiah 33:3

If any of you lacks wisdom, he should ask God, who gives generously to all without finding fault, and it will be given to him.

- James 1:5

Your impact on others is limited only by your imagination, drive, passion, persistence, talent, and time. Why do so many people volunteer to help other, less-fortunate people? Well, it really is better to give than receive. To have actually helped another person and made that person's life a little better, easier, or happier is a tremendously gratifying feeling. As many have observed, it is often hard to tell who received the greater benefit – the recipient or the volunteer who gave his time, attention, effort, or money.

Our ultimate example of impact on others is of course, Jesus. He is our perfect model. If each of us could only have a tiny fraction of the impact Christ had (and has), that impact would be enormous. God created each of us uniquely and instilled different talents in each of us. He has graced us with gifts. Each of us needs to be on a mission to find those gifts and use them!

If we live as Christ-like as humanly possible, continuing to make course corrections and resets as needed (which will be often), and realize and take action on the amazing truth that God knows us individually and gave each of us talents to use for abundance and for His glory, we can accomplish far greater things and have far greater impact on others than we could ever have imagined.

Remember the verse from Jeremiah 17:7? ("But blessed is the man who trusts in the Lord, whose confidence is in him.")

Remember Paul's advice to rejoice in the Lord and to take our requests to God for a peace beyond understanding? (Philippians 4:4-7.)

Remember the admonitions in Ephesians to get rid of anger and bitterness and embrace compassion and love? (Ephesians 4:31-32; Ephesians 5:1-2.)

God tells us, if we take these actions, He will partner with us, just as He did with Randall Wallace.

Remember these verses from Psalms?

Delight yourself in the Lord and he will give you the desires of your heart.

Commit your way to the Lord; trust in him and he will do this: He will make your righteousness shine like the dawn, the justice of your cause like the noonday sun.

Be still before the Lord and wait patiently for him; do not fret when men succeed in their ways, when they carry out their wicked schemes.

Refrain from anger and turn from wrath; do not fret – it leads only to evil. For evil men will be cut off, but those who hope in the Lord will inherit the land.

If the Lord delights in a man's way, he makes his steps firm; though he stumble, he will not fall, for the Lord upholds him with his hand.

- Psalm 37:4-9 and 23-24

That's as inspirational as it gets! Let's follow Paul's instruction to cast aside all timidity (2 Timothy 1:6-7) and get busy! Daily walks help me understand these truths and inspire and motivate me to act on this realization. I encourage you to do the same, while we still have time on this earth. Go for it. Start somewhere. See where it leads.

Remember, a journey of a thousand miles begins with one step. Take that step. Start imagining. Start using your talents. Watch for and act on "tap moments" that come your way. Co-labor with God. Resolve to make a difference, every day.

God is extending His hand of partnership to each of us. Accept the grace of His gifts. Take His hand. Walk with Him on what will be surely be an amazing journey!

CHAPTER TWELVE

ONE LIFE TO LIVE

Teach us to number our days aright, that we may gain a heart of wisdom.

Relent, O Lord! How long will it be? Have compassion on your servants.

Satisfy us in the morning with your unfailing love, that we may sing for joy and be glad all our days.

Make us glad for as many days as you have afflicted us, for as many years as we have seen trouble.

May your deeds be shown to your servants, your splendor to their children.

May the favor of the Lord our God rest upon us; establish the work of our hands for us — yes, establish the work of our hands.

- Psalm 90:12-17

"I'll start tomorrow."

"I'll get to that later, when the timing is better."

"I have plenty of time."

If you're a young person, take heed: you don't have forever. It seems as though you do, but time flies faster than you imagine it will. Ten years from now, you'll be saying, "where did the time go?" I know, because it happened to me. Readers who are in their 50s or 60s, and certainly those older, and even those in their 40s, can relate.

By all means, explore the world, enjoy life, have fun! None of those things poses a conflict with the idea of starting early to think about your talents, and what you want to do with your life beyond day-to-day functionality – about the bigger picture, how you want to make a difference and "outlive" yourself. Even about how to live more richly in your daily routine. By "more richly" I mean more fully, more deeply, more satisfyingly, in your relationships and interactions with family, friends, and the world around you.

I've never forgotten the large inscription above the stage

in the study hall at McCallie, the boarding school I attended my last three years of high school, in Chattanooga, Tennessee. I recall the room as big and old, in a big, old brick building. But mostly I recall that inscription:

Man's Chief End is to Glorify God and Enjoy Him Forever.

I didn't know it at the time, but that statement is the answer to the first question ("What is the chief end of man?") of the Westminster Shorter Catechism (written in 1646 – 1647 by a group of English and Scottish theologians and laymen). Apparently, the purpose was to educate children and others of "weaker capacity" in the Reformed faith (based on the teachings of John Calvin). Based on that stated purpose, we can use the education, too, over 350 years later, here in the 21st century. We should have childlike faith . . . and frankly, most of us are closer to the "weaker capacity" end of the spectrum than the "stronger capacity" end (I'm not sure who's on the strong side beyond Billy Graham and a few others).

God wants us to succeed. By "succeed" I mean maximize our talents to create abundance and joy for ourselves, our loved ones, and others, in a way that shines the light of Christ as a beacon, and in a way that glorifies God.

God wants us to communicate with Him, to enjoy Him. Not live in fear. Sure, His power and omniscience are scary on one level, partly because we can't comprehend or fully understand. We are, even as adults, like children. We believe by faith. We seek answers to prayers. We listen for His voice.

When we understand and embrace that God, in all His power and omniscience, made each of us specially, wonderfully, and wants a relationship with us, has a plan for each of us, and will and does bless us in countless ways, we experience a bewildering mix of exhilaration, trepidation, confusion, self-doubt, and assurance.

Exhilaration . . . that God created each of us for a purpose, is watching over us, and is available for consultations at any and every moment of our lives.

Trepidation because . . . what if we mess up? What if we can't get a clear picture of our purposes in life, why we are here?

Confusion . . . about where to start, what to do, how to make the right choices.

Self-doubt . . . because how can we measure up to God's standards? How can each of us be so special? How can we turn our lives around after repeated failures?

Assurance . . . *because we realize God loves us no matter what.* He knows we're human. He knows we'll stumble. We know He's there to pick us up, dust us off, and nudge us back on the path with words of encouragement. We know He will walk with us each step of the way, through the valley, the swamp, the mud, the rain, into the sunshine, over the rocks, all the way to the mountaintop. In the toughest spots, we may stumble, but God will grab our hands before we fall. That is blessed assurance.

The daily walks bring into crystal-clear focus that each of us has one life to live. God has given each of us a finite number of days on this earth. Only He knows how many.

Wake up each morning with gratitude. You woke up! You're alive! Start the day with a smile! Another day to be a shining light, to make a difference, big or small. What a blessing!

Instead of complaining about how early is it, how bad the weather is, the dog missing the potty paper, breakfast not being how you like it, your child not listening the first time, bad drivers or bad traffic, how Sally or Bob hurt your feelings, blah blah blah . . .

Be thankful you're still here . . .

Be thankful you have a family who loves you . . .

Be thankful you have gifts from God (children and other gifts!) . . .

Be thankful you can walk outside to watch the sunrise, feel the breeze on your face, watch birds fly and squirrels play, hear the laughter of a young child . . .

Be thankful your mind is sharp . . .

Be thankful you have the ability to smile and say "good morning" to a stranger . . .

Be thankful you have yet another day to continue (or start!) using your talents for good . . .

Be thankful you have time to apologize to a family member or someone else you hurt by your words or actions yesterday . . .

Be thankful you can make someone else feel special today . . .

Be thankful you can help someone else in need today . . .

Be thankful you have another opportunity to change your life for the better, to eliminate bad habits, to start new habits, to paint a picture, to write a story, to take a hot meal to a home-bound elderly person, to be ready for the "tap" . . .

Be thankful you're still in the game . . .

Be thankful God has given you another day to make a difference!

Take that walk. Clear your mind. Have the wonderment of a child. Laugh often. Feel the breeze. Watch the animals play. Greet the passersby. Smile. Slow down, be still. Listen for God's voice. Have a conversation with Him about your purpose in life, why He created you. Experience the joy that He knows you, is with you, and will help you. Challenge yourself to commit to action, follow your purpose, shine that light.

As you walk, release any anger or envy. Let God lift you out of any misery. Don't inflict your misery onto others. Instead, look to them for support and encouragement. Be happy for their happiness and success. Learn from them. Maybe God has put them into your path for a reason.

Realize that Zero Sum is a loser's game. God, I imagine, shakes His head in disappointment at those wasted lives, wasted talents. If only . . . don't be one of the "if onlys."

Join the walk into renewal. Shed the old skin. Be revitalized daily. Let go of all the negatives. *God is in control.* Stop fighting Him. You can't win that battle. Humble yourself. Ask for His guidance. Ask for His will to be done.

Pray for healing, and know He hears you and will do what's best. Sometimes that's enough for a miracle, as we experienced with our son Josh's dramatic turnaround from the edge of death to survival and recovery.

How would it have ended if Nancy had not humbled herself? Had she not released her anger at God? Had she not acknowledged only He was in control? Had she not acknowledged Josh's life was in His hands? Had she not prayed for His will to be done? Had she not arrived at a profound peace about whatever He decided for Josh?

I don't know. Only God knows. But I am so grateful for Nancy's unceasing prayers in the chapel. I am beyond grateful to God for sending a messenger "angel" to Nancy to tell her He heard her . . . and for saving Josh's life.

Go generate your spiritual, emotional, and creative energy packets. Walk with a newfound purpose. Use the energy in whatever amazing ways God has planned for you. *Be the light.* Watch the effect on your family, your friends, and the bigger world around you. Most of all, watch the effect on you.

It doesn't matter if you're 15, 35, 60, or 80. A new day is dawning. Put on your walking shoes. Get out there. Watch the sky began to glow. Watch the sun rise. Let your light shine, in so many ways. Give God a reason to smile as

He watches you walk . . . run . . . soar. He's right beside you!

> *Do you not know? Have you not heard? The Lord is the everlasting God, the Creator of the ends of the earth. He will not grow tired or weary, and his understanding no one can fathom.*
>
> *He gives strength to the weary and increases the power of the weak.*
>
> *Even youths grow tired and weary, and young men stumble and fall; but those who hope in the Lord will renew their strength.*
>
> *They will soar on wings like eagles; they will run and not grow weary, they will walk and not be faint.*
>
> - Isaiah 40:28-31

We each have one life to live. What will you make of the rest of yours?

Walk with God.

Every day will be a blessing, in ways untold, beyond imagination.

See you at the river.

Notes

NOTES

NOTES

NOTES

Made in the USA
Lexington, KY
07 April 2019